The School I'd Like

Do our schools really meet the needs of children and young people today?

'No one reading this collection will be left with any doubt that children and young people are capable and entitled to help shape their present and future.'

(from the Preface)

In 2001 the *Guardian* launched a competition called 'The School I'd Like', in which young people were asked to imagine their ideal school. This vibrant, ground-breaking book presents material drawn from that competition, offering a unique snapshot of perceptions of today's schools by those who matter most – the pupils.

The book is wonderfully illustrated by children's essays, stories, poems, pictures and plans. Placing their views in the centre of the debate, it provides an evaluation of the democratic processes involved in teaching and learning by:

- identifying consistencies in children's expressions of how they wish to learn;
- highlighting particular sites of 'disease' in the education system today;
- illustrating how the built environment is experienced by today's children;
- posing questions about the reconstruction of teaching and learning for the twenty-first century.

This book offers a powerful new perspective on school reform and will be essential reading for all those involved in education and childhood studies, including teachers, advisors, policy-makers, and academics, and anyone who believes that children's voices should not be ignored.

Catherine Burke is Lecturer in Education at the School of Education, University of Leeds. **Ian Grosvenor** is Director of Learning and Teaching at the School of Education, University of Birmingham.

The School I'd Like

Children and young people's reflections on an education for the 21st century

Catherine Burke and Ian Grosvenor

with an Afterword by Dea Birkett

RoutledgeFalmer
Taylor & Francis Group

LONDON AND NEW YORK

First published 2003 by RoutledgeFalmer
11 New Fetter Lane, London EC4P 4EE

Simultaneously published in the USA and Canada
by RoutledgeFalmer
29 West 35th Street, New York, NY 10001

RoutledgeFalmer is an imprint of the Taylor & Francis Group

© 2003 Catherine Burke and Ian Grosvenor

Typeset in Times by Wearset Ltd, Boldon, Tyne and Wear
Printed and bound in Great Britain by TJ International Ltd, Padstow, Cornwall

British Library Cataloguing in Publication Data
A catalogue record for this book is available from the British Library

Library of Congress Cataloging in Publication Data
A catalog record has been requested

ISBN 0–415–30115–7 (pb)
   0–415–30114–9 (hb)

Dedicated to all those children who raised their voice and to the memory of Edward Blishen, Brian Simon, Caroline Benn and all who have fought for a better and fairer school system for children and young people in the UK

Contents

PART 4
Flexible contexts   **119**

Foreword

Becky Gardiner
Former editor of the *Education Guardian*

As editor of the *Guardian*'s Education supplement I was used to politicians, pundits and press releases all claiming to offer the solution to some educational 'problem' or other. But nothing could have prepared me for this. 'The School I'd Like' competition unleashed the most imaginative and provocative challenges to our education system I had seen. And they all came from children. We launched the competition after Catherine Burke sent a letter asking for help with a project she was running. She wanted to hear what children felt about their schooling, and wondered if we knew about a competition our sister paper, the *Observer*, had run in 1967 asking children to design the school of their dreams. I dug out the original from the archives, and was immediately persuaded to run the competition again. The entries would be given to the School of Education at the University of Leeds, thereby creating an archive of children's views on education. The 1967 competition attracted almost 1,000 entries. We did not expect to get as many.

We worried that the pressures of a national curriculum would prevent teachers and pupils reflecting on what was wrong with the way things were, or 'wasting time' by planning for the seemingly impossible. We were wrong; with their teachers' help, thousands of children from hundreds of schools found time to dream.

Few proposed no school, though many wanted less school and every child wanted a better school. Some ideas appeared the stuff of pure fantasy: a school in a submarine, with waterproof maps of the underwater world; private helicopters to fly children to France for double French; voice-activated pencils. Others seemed more prosaic: swimming pools, a jug of water in every classroom; enough books and computers to go round; chill-out rooms. But all the ideas went some way to answering the really important questions about education: what is good about schools today, and what could be improved? How can we turn schools into places where children happily go, and are able to learn? And what is education *for* anyway?

Some people will no doubt dismiss their criticisms as trivial, as merely reflecting the silly preoccupations of children. They would be wrong. Take toilets, for example. Nearly every entry mentioned them. They were smelly and dirty and the locks never worked. They wished that paper and soap were provided so they could wash their hands. But who says this is a trivial issue? Several thoroughly 'grown-up' studies have shown that unpleasant toilets encourage bullying and contribute to truancy. Worse, they show a disregard for the dignity of pupils.

'Respect' was the single word that occurred most; it was what the children wanted, but felt they didn't get. They were forced to do work they weren't interested in, in buildings that were falling down around their ears. They were expected to fit into a structure and a curriculum that seemed to have been created without the first reference to what they might enjoy, or respond to. Most of all, they were sick of not being listened to. Sick of being treated like kids.

I hope that this book will give people an opportunity to listen to children. I hope that educators, architects and politicians will read it, and find inspiration. And I hope that we will not have to wait another three decades before anyone thinks to listen to children, and act on what they say.

Preface

Over the past decade, the notion that teaching and learning are fundamental to improving the world has become heresy as the teaching profession has succumbed to overwhelming pressure to conform to market forces, and attendant measures of productivity, competition and accountability. The school, rather than the crucible of morality, justice and values, has become regarded as a mechanism of objective instruction, stripped of its moral or political function. The academy has become associated with distanced measurement rather than embroiled in arguments about the urgency of radical revision or reform. All this has occurred without consulting children themselves, now considered along with their parents, as clients and educational consumers.

This volume represents a challenge to these tendencies. It places the voices of children aged between 5 and 18 years at the centre of a critique of education today. It sets these voices, recorded during a three-month period in early 2001, alongside the voices of children recorded in 1967, who were all responding to the same task: to describe or design 'The School I'd Like'.

In the heady days of the late 1960s, children, alongside other social groups, were beginning to be considered as part of the oppressed and agents of their own destiny. A collection of writing by secondary school children, edited by Edward Blishen and published by Penguin Books in 1969, forms the backdrop to the present volume. Blishen's book was the inspiration for this volume and for the return to the competition in association with the *Guardian* newspaper. Although the recent contributions are more numerous than those Blishen worked with, the present authors have faced the same dilemmas in sifting through the thousands of entries. Like Blishen, we were presented with a sustained, articulate and sober exposition of reasoning for a radical reconsideration of the purpose and possibilities of education; a considered plea for a 'new order' in our schools and a rejoicing in the opportunity to help shape this new order.

Set with the task of shaping this volume, the authors had, unlike Blishen, the unique opportunity to consider comparatively the responses of children to the same question over time. The specific conditions under which the task was presented to children both in 1967 and in 2001 are unknown. Many entries to the competition in both cases were clearly influenced by teachers who provided a structure for the exercise. The task to write an essay on 'the ideal school' or 'what you would change about school' was in many cases set as homework. As Blishen noted in the introduction to his volume, sometimes the guidance by teachers was rather deadening in effect. On opening the envelopes containing large numbers of entries to the recent competition, one recognised almost immediately whether or not a free hand had been given to the youngsters. A pack containing thirty-six 'recipes' of 'ingredients' for a 'good' school told us more about the teacher and perhaps even the school than the ideas of the children.

It was the *Observer* newspaper that sponsored the competition in 1967, which received 943 entries. This competition had as its focus the future of the secondary school. In 2001, the *Observer*'s sister newspaper, the *Guardian*, agreed to host the competition and received multiple entries from over 1,500 schools and hundreds of individuals. Categories used in the 2001 competition were primary (ages 4–11), lower secondary (ages 11–16) and upper secondary (ages 16–18). Sometimes the precise age was not given in class or group entries; sometimes the name of the child was not included. Usually, one class or one school year participated; sometimes a whole school took part. This time, the focus was the future of school itself and entries came from across the whole of the UK, from inner-city reception classes to rural comprehensives. They came from those who had very little and whose school was situated within run-down communities, whose children were the last in a long line of generations who had gained nothing from schooling. Pinned to these entries were explanations from teachers who pointed out that their needs were so great that they had concentrated on the basics such as warmth and light. They came from the independent sector where basic needs were still not met, such as locks on the toilet doors. They came from special schools and hospital education units for whom the usual boundaries of age as used in the competition did not apply. The home educated took the opportunity to participate in the debate and the traveller community was represented by one entry which asked that school might follow him around the country.

What is presented here is only a fraction of the archive but it offers a detailed 'snapshot' of how school was regarded by children and young people across the UK in the early months of 2001. The collection, including essays, pictures, stories, plays, designs, plans, poems, film and photography, raises questions about how teaching and learning could be reconstructed in the twenty-first century. It expresses children's own ways of seeing and naming issues of concern to all involved in education. It illuminates ways in which the built environment is understood and experienced by school-age children. Particular sites of 'disease' in the system, its infrastructure and everyday practice are highlighted and the ways that 'pupil' perspectives are incorporated into school and school reform are problematised. The possibilities of reconceiving 'school' and redesigning platforms for learning are explored. The discussion of this rich set of comparative data, set at the head of each chapter, identifies consistencies across time in the expressed ways that children and young people wish to learn. However, these texts will always be open to interpretation from different points of view. They will merit revisiting as new or different questions are asked about the condition of childhood and education in the future.

The materials we have selected could have been organised differently. In making sense of the vast quantity and variety of responses, like Blishen before us, we have drawn up themes which seemed to arise from the data and connect with emerging research agendas. A major difference between the two collections is that the visual dimension, which was acknowledged but not used by Blishen, is accorded in this

collection equal significance with written texts. As historians we are always interested in the relationship between the past, the present and the future and have read
the material accordingly. That said, we have identified the first name, age and place
of each contributor to enable the reader to look for different perspectives, for
example how age and gender shapes perception.

These voices are the voices of history. They tell us as much as any history of post-
1970 schooling published in the UK, because they go beyond policy and the administrative and engage with education as experienced. The texts, drawings and other
material contributions gathered here allow for a view of the world not visible to
many in a position to make and implement policy about schooling. The children
address contemporary educational issues but the language and images they choose
are critical of their experiences of schooling and contemporary education. The
routine rhetoric of judgement and demarcation such as 'special needs', 'excellence',
'gifted and talented', 'raising standards', 'target setting', 'failing schools' and 'school
improvement' are recognised by them but are seen as bounded and divisive and
counter to ideas of equality, fairness and justice as they experience and understand
them.

No one reading this collection will be left feeling content that the education
system in the UK is meeting the needs of children and young people today. No one
reading the collection will be left with any doubt that children and young people are
capable and entitled to help to shape their present and future and, as Edward
Blishen commented with his 1967 children in mind, 'No one will read this selection
without feeling some shame at what we have done to these children. Who will
answer them? Who will explain to them why they should not have what they
demand?'

Acknowledgements

We would like to thank all of the children, teachers, parents and others, past and present, who participated in the competitions and the construction of the 2001 archive; the *Guardian* newspaper for hosting the competition and for handling, with skill, the enormous response; Dea Birkett for 'The Children's Manifesto'; Toshiba for providing the prizes; Tim Brighouse, Gus Gilder, John Clifford, Lee Hall and Becky Gardiner for judging the competition; Dea Birkett for covering the competition so sensitively in her *Guardian* features and the University of Leeds for storing the archive. We would also like to thank participants in the EERA History of Education network, the International Standing Conference for the History of Education and the Domus seminar series at the University of Birmingham for stimulating discussion throughout the development of this project. Special thanks to Kate Rousmaniere, Ning de Coninck Smith and Mark Dudek for generous encouragement and critical reading of drafts.

Thanks to Susan Daniels at the University of Leeds for generous support and encouragement and to Rosa Hall, Jean Roebuck and Andrea Peel for clerical support.

Finally, thank you to Rowan and Anna for providing evidence every day of the endless possibilities and hundreds of ways of being a child.

All participating children, where possible, have been approached and agreed to allow their words and images to be used in the book.

Introduction
Neglected voices

If people are to secure and maintain a democratic way of life, they must have opportunities to learn what that way of life means and how it might be led.

John Dewey, 1916

... to alienate men [sic] from their own decision-making is to change them into objects.

Paulo Freire, 1996

My ideal school is no school.

Robert, 12, 2001

An often-observed characteristic of the history of education in the UK is the fact that, in spite of regular overhauling of policy and practice through national legislation, so much of the experience for children and their teachers stays the same. Commentators have sought to explain this 'continuity in pedagogical practice', across sites and over time and have located it in the 'power relations, in educational institutions and processes, that remain untouched by the majority of curriculum and other reforms' (Gore, 2001: 167). Part of the powerful mythology of school is the notion that it can be altered, changed and improved, that reasons for past failures have been identified and that the school of the near future will not resemble the past. Developments in educational technology, especially in the application and use of computers in learning, have given further credence to the message, carried in recent government policy rhetoric, that schools can be 'transformed' (DfES, 2002). The belief, held by young people that it is possible and vital to transform schools was certainly present in Blishen's selection.

Children have changed and schools should! A school should be filled with the amenities and inventions of our century. It should teach children more about the future and less about the past.

Lynda, 16

∽∽∽

There will be no classrooms in their schools, no bells to interrupt. They will never shrink from the dreaded thoughts of exams: exams for them will not exist.

Johanna, 16

However, this optimistic belief that schools will be different is tempered in the 2001 data with an understanding of how schools work as institutions which control pupils' lives. Many children offer a realistic appraisal of the possibilities for change and betray a weary acceptance of what they consider to be the inevitability of continuity of organisational structures. The following is from the 2001 data:

> Even in the 21st century in schools pupils sit in rows like the Victorians. You can only talk to the person next to you (this is probably why the teachers make us sit in rows) this means that in discussion work which is extremely important in today's society ideas and suggestions don't come as quickly.
>
> Joanna, 13, Wokingham

It is clear that children and young people have yet to be convinced that their right to have a say is genuinely respected. Today, the young are subject to frequent and regular consultation and questioning, their views, tastes and inclinations surveyed and sampled. In contrast to their counterparts in 1967, who showed a genuine belief in the inevitable transformation of school and the value of their own contribution to the task, the 2001 data reflects a certain amount of resignation that they might be consulted but never actually permitted to take part in the challenge of changing school. Ticking boxes may help formulate policy but never changes anything. Schooling remains an experience to be endured, an experience which, when it does offer enjoyment, is mainly because it is a place where children are able to meet their friends (Barnados, 1996; Christensen and James, 2001).

In the UK and other developed and post-industrialised societies, there has since the early 1990s been a build up of structures that involve children and young people in political decision-making, for example the European Youth Parliament; national youth parliaments in the Caribbean and New Zealand; and, other more localised structures in cities and towns across Europe (Wyness, 2002). This concern with hearing the voices of young people in the political decision-making policy processes has been accompanied in the UK by policy actions involving a greater acknowledgement of children's rights, autonomy and self-regulation. This international and national policy shift can be directly related to the establishment of the United Nations Convention on the Rights of the Child (UN, 1989) and an increased recognition within the research and policy communities that children are not invisible, but social actors involved in the construction and negotiation of social order.

Articles 12 to 15 of the UNCRC affirm children's right to freedom of expression, right to information, freedom of thought, conscience and religion, and the right to freedom of association (UN, 1989). The UNCRC came into force in the UK in January 1991. The Convention requires governments to report to the UN Committee on the Rights of the Child details of implementation two years after ratification and every five years subsequently. The UK's second report was submitted in 1999. The Blair government and its devolved administrations have put in place 'mechanisms' to create a 'new landscape' for the 15 million children aged 0–19 in the UK and to ensure 'a more strategic and coherent approach to children's issues across Government'. In England a new Cabinet Committee for Children and Young People was established in 2000, the post of Minister for Children and Young People was created and a cross-government children's unit established (UK *Implementation*, 2002: paragraphs 2, 5 and 15). In 2001 the Labour government's

Children and Young People's Unit launched its consultation document, *Building a Strategy for Children and Young People* to gather views on a strategic approach to children's provision. Between November 2001 and March 2002, some 2,500 children and young people responded to the 'Your Say' consultation exercise. Respondents were asked to structure their thoughts around several listed themes. The majority of the responses revolved around 'Achievement and Enjoyment' and many of these comments were linked to experience of schooling (*Your Say*, 2002). Also in 2001 the Government launched *Core Principles for Involving Young People in Government*. This was a commitment that Departments in England responsible directly for policies and services for children and young people would operate against clear principles and would produce annually reviewed action plans (UK *Implementation*, 2002: paras 15, 28). In the summer of 2002 the Department for Education and Skills (DfES) issued its action plan *Listening to Learn*.

Parallel to these policy actions in the UK and elsewhere is recognition amongst researchers and policy-makers that childhood has changed. These changes are in large measure the unplanned consequence of wider change in developed and post-industrial societies. Research and theorising are rendering children visible in public spaces (Wyness, 2000). Children and young people, rather than being passive subjects of social structures, are coming to be recognised as being active in shaping their social identities and as competent members of society whose voices should be heard (James, Jenks and Prout, 1998). So, for example, in 1999 the Qualifications and Curriculum Authority (QCA) commissioned the National Forum for Educational Research to conduct a review of research that involved directly asking pupils about their experiences of, and attitudes to, the National Curriculum since its introduction in 1989. Studies conducted in Northern Ireland and Scotland were considered alongside research in England and Wales (Lord and Harland, 2000). However, the most significant research development in the UK has been the ESRC funded *Children 5–16 Growing into the 21st Century*. This programme attempted to uncover how the world looks from the perspective of children. A series of projects, both large and small scale, have produced surveys of structural factors shaping contemporary childhood and produced in-depth qualitative and ethnographic studies of children's daily social interactions. The programme produced evidence and overwhelming support for children's voices to be heard and for extending the means by which they can participate in the institutions associated with their everyday lives, particularly schools.

The value of listening to pupils' views on schooling is, to paraphrase Lord and Harland, 'obvious – they experience [it] first hand' (2000: 6) and as Cullingford observed, 'Children ... have the articulateness and honesty to analyse what they experience ... listening to children makes us consider some of the habits we have taken for granted' (Cullingford, 1991: 2). The Cantle inquiry team in their report on the 2001 urban riots in the north of England further reinforced these observations on the importance of listening to young people:

> [we were] particularly struck by the views of younger people, who, in strong terms, emphasised the need to break down barriers by promoting knowledge and understanding of different cultures. Younger people were seen to be leading the process of transition and should be given every encouragement to develop it further.
>
> (Cantle Inquiry, 2002: 30)

In sum, as already indicated, there is a growing body of research and published literature on the subject of children as active and competent members of society (see, for example, Alderson, 1995, 2000a; Griffiths, 1998; Treseder, 1997; Wilson, 1999; Walker, 2001). It should be noted at this point that asking children for their views is not new. For example, in 1939, Mass Observation carried out a school survey in the East End of London on anti-semitism, obtaining brief essays from a range of boys and girls. Mass Observation believed that childhood was a critical stage in the formation of attitudes towards minority groups (Kushner, 1995: 6). In 1948 Cecil Stewart in *The Village Surveyed* described a participatory study of Sutton-at-Hone in Kent where local children were asked to produce essays on 'My Plan for My Village'. This activity was part of a strategy to cultivate citizenship and reconstruct community life after the Second World War (Matless, 1998: 236–7). A similar concern for engaging young people in thinking about the future was behind the annual school essay competition organised in the 1950s by the Council for Visual Education on themes such as 'My favourite Street' and 'Beautiful Buildings I have Seen' (Matless, 1998: 260).

To return to the present, despite policy changes, the establishment of specialist units, new research agendas and a 'common sense' recognition of the value of listening and acting upon the voices of children and young people, it is evident that as social actors they still feel controlled by adults and that their views are not being heard (Mayall, 2000; Edwards, Alldred and David, 2002).

In English education law, schooling is seen a 'contract between school and parents', a contract which does not include children (DfEE, 1999: para 7). This contract can be seen as being in direct contravention of the UNCRC, but as Lee (1999) has pointed out the rights enshrined in UNCRC are couched in terms of the individual child's competence, with 'giving due weight' in accordance with the age and maturity of the child in effect placing children's agency in the determining control of adults. The UK government is committed to its obligations under the UNCRC: children's 'voices must be heard at the heart of Government' (UK *Implementation*, 2002: para 25). This commitment involved developing a 'shared, collective vision of parents, carers, the voluntary sector, the statutory sector, Government – and children and young people themselves' which would provide indicators to measure success in a range of outcomes 'health and well-being; achievement; participation and citizenship; protection; responsibility and inclusion'. However, a shared vision does not necessarily mean that all who endorse it are necessarily equal partners. In the *Your Say* consultation it was adults who selected the themes about which questions would be asked. In other words, responsible adults determined the agenda for children's agency. Children and young people can be asked, but they remain apprentice citizens, rather than fully constituted members of the social and political world. This is explicit in the DfES *Listening to Learn* (2002) action plan. 'Children and young people' it states 'at the heart of the Department's strategy *Delivering Results*':

> Our vision is for a department which is young-person friendly and accessible, responsive to their needs and aspirations, and renowned throughout government for leading change in involving children and young people.

Achieving this vision would 'help us to deliver better services to children and young people, including the hardest to reach and those facing disadvantage and inequality, to raise standards for all and to promote personal and social development'.

School and schooling are presented as a given within a conceptual framework of school reform and improvement. The plan is about working through existing structures and is framed in terms of 'We will' phrases – We will 'collect', 'introduce', 'launch', 'consult and work with', 'report on', 'gather' and 'involve'. It is adults, though, who will mediate children's worlds as the last few lines of the plan make explicit: 'But we alone will not set the agenda. Through surveying the opinions of children and young people *we will identify* the matters which they regard as important' (our emphasis).

At the local level of schools, a review of the research on the success of school councils as mechanisms for promoting student views and institutional change points to a high level of student dissatisfaction. *A Child's View of School* (NSPCC, 1995) reported that students often felt that a school council gave a surface appearance of involvement rather than genuinely reflecting an institutional interest in students' views. Alderson (2000b), researching UK students' views on children's rights, found that less than a fifth of 2,272 students aged 7–17 reported that they had an effective school council, and that many students reported feeling that teachers did not listen to them very much, or take account of their views, or trust them to make decisions. Wyse (2001), in a small-scale study of children's participation, found that opportunities for students to express their views and feel they were being listened to were very limited, even when school councils were in place. Other evidence, admittedly, offers some corrective to this picture of dissatisfaction. Hepburn (1984), writing about research findings based on five studies in the USA, concluded that 'democratic experiences in the school and the classroom do contribute to the participatory awareness, skills and attitudes fundamental to life in democratic societies' (Hepburn, 1984: 261). Davies (1998) found, in a case study of ten UK schools, that school councils helped to reduce pupil exclusions. It is useful to be reminded here that the UK government's desire to place children's 'voices at the heart of government' is explicitly linked in policy objectives with tackling social exclusion (UK *Implementation*, 2002). Further research is clearly needed, especially in the context of the concern expressed by Walker (2001) about the effectiveness of the instruments currently used in research to ascertain evidence of the perceptions of children and young people about the services they receive.

To this data on dissatisfaction, other research evidence relating to schooling must be added. In both 1967 and 2001, young people were critical of the demands placed upon them by the examinations system. Yet, since the introduction of the National Curriculum, the level of testing has increased enormously and significantly distorts the learning experiences of school students, as one commentator observed in 2001: 'the kids think they do the learning for their teachers nowadays, so they get good results for the school, not for themselves' (Birkett, 2001: 2). Butterfield (1993) and Davies and Brember (1997, 1999) have presented research evidence of how the introduction of national assessment across the key stages in England created stress and anxiety amongst pupils and contributed to a drop in self-esteem amongst some of them. There is also evidence that the enjoyment of school declines sharply as children get older (HEA, 1999: passim; Lord and Harland, 2000: 50–1) and that the levels of occasional and long-term truancy are indicators of acute disengagement from schooling (Social Exclusion Unit, 1998; Klein, 2000).

In a recent essay on learning and 'getting an education' Jay Lemke wrote about the old saying that 'it takes a village to raise a child'. He argued that children know how they need to learn 'about everything and everyone in our communities' to live there successfully and as they learnt they 'gradually become our villages', internalising the diversity of viewpoints that collectively makes sense of all that goes on in the community. During this process, children 'developed values and identities' (Lemke, 2002: 34). Lemke's essay provides a useful starting point for thinking about schools and schooling in the twenty-first century.

In the journey to 'become our village', participation in socially meaningful activities is about both what is learnt and how it is learnt. The contents of our thinking and the habits of our lives originate in our social interactions with others. School is the first environment after home – indeed probably the first public space – with which children identify, have a sense of belonging and are familiar. Schools act as a setting, a source for formal and informal learning experiences, where children learn to be members of a group, to engage in social discourse and relations, and to adapt to more formal kinds of trust and rights than experienced in the home. Schooling represents an ordered passage from child to adult status and within this public community of intimate strangers, adults, in the minority but acting on the behalf of parents, control and regulate the activity of the majority, children. Control is in the buildings, the space created, and in the material contents of this space – furniture and equipment. It is in the order imposed on the bodies in this space (Markus, 1996). Children, through rules (which by their very nature imply, both symbolically and in practice, a sense of mistrust), conventions and institutional practice, have their lives regularised. They are segregated with their peers according to age and levels of attainment and sequentially progress through regulated structures. The school day is structured into timetabled units and cultural knowledge orientated towards the values and norms of society at large is transmitted to new generations. In sum, the present-day institution of school, its design and use, is a critical factor in the journey 'to become our village'. However, as Lemke notes, while the values and norms that schools transmit may reflect the community outside, schools exist as unique 'micro-villages in their own right, with their own typical activities' separated from the 'larger village' (Lemke, 2002: 43).

A passionate desire to be heard and a remarkable capacity of resistance to the total culture of school stands as a powerful link between the voices recorded in Blishen's study and those generated by the 2001 competition. The following voices are taken from Blishen.

> At last we have been consulted. I, an average fifteen-year-old public schoolgirl, am now allowed to voice my opinion on the school that I would like.
>
> Judith, 15

〰〰〰

> My main complaint is that we have so little say in school affairs.
>
> S (boy), 15

〰〰〰

My need is now, today ... Teach me not to be apathetic, share your wisdom, listen to my ideals.

Susan, 16

∞∞∞

I don't think I would get on very well in my ideal school because I am too used to being told what to do.

Frances, 15

∞∞∞

The fault with a lot of schools today is that teachers are not prepared to listen ... They don't mind discussing various topics as long as it ends up with them being able to prove a point to you and not the other way.

Lyne, 15

The next three extracts are from the 2001 data:

To see the problems about schools you have to see through the appearance and into what may even be the depression of the children experiencing school. They know the problems. The adults need to listen to them and not dismiss their opinions.

James, 12, Loughborough

∞∞∞

I'm an English teenager living in the country of my birth as much of an English citizen as those who control this country. I have no voice of my own education, I am doomed to be pushed around by faceless politicians and never listened to until I am of voting age. Even then I will have hardly any say in my own country. We, as people who have spent almost every year of our lives being told what to do by teachers, governors, etc. should have some say in how our school's run.

Angela, 15, Croydon

∞∞∞

In my ideal school ... we will no longer be treated like herds of an identical animal waiting to be civilised before we are let loose on the world. It will be recognised that it is our world too.

Miriam, 15, Reading

These examples show how widely children, young people, their teachers, parents, guardians and friends have interpreted the task to describe their preferred school or education. The meaning of school, its purpose and functions, its place in individual lives, the community and the world are on the agenda. No tick box survey could solicit such a creative and critical response, the scope and ambition of which has as usual reminded us of the capabilities of young people in helping to design their worlds. The anger at not being heard is regularly complemented by practical suggestions for change, usually centring on the development of more democratic structures, especially the use of School Councils. Again, a few extracts from the data will suffice; the first five are taken from Blishen, the rest from the 2001 data:

The pupils would organize the running of the school along with the staff so the school was more the sort of place the pupils wanted it to be. Due to this scheme the pupils would take a more lively interest in the activities of the school as they would choose and organize them (with some help from the staff) themselves.

Ruth, 15

〰〰

I would like to see a student committee, with representatives for junior and senior parts of the school, in order to lobby the headmaster if anything (including teaching methods) was unsatisfactory. (If juniors found complaints, they should first be considered by chosen members of the sixth form.)

Alan, 16

〰〰

I would like to see self-government by the pupils. I suggest a sort of committee made up of pupils of each age group and elected by that group. To this committee could go grievances and complaints. At a weekly (or fortnightly) meeting of the whole school these would be dealt with and punishment meted out by the committee.

Susan, 16

〰〰

Present-day schools are run by groups of people who don't really know the essentials of school problems. The people most directly concerned with the problems are never consulted. In the ideal school a group of the older boys and girls should be chosen by the other children as representatives, and this group should take over the duties of the governors. The children should, therefore, under the guidance of the head teacher, be virtually running the school themselves.

Brian, 16

〰〰

. . . as at colleges and universities, there would be a Students' Union.

Ian, 17

〰〰

As pupils we are able to create
An atmosphere of freedom.
We are willing and eager
To express our thoughts
Our school is a place where
Children are free to be a child.

Jayne, 8, Altringham

〰〰

Instead of an authority structure which destroys decision making and a sense of responsibility, and which outside the classroom can prove outright dangerous, priority is given to structuring relationships such that children can talk to adults, can lean on and trust adults, can ask things of adults, can in short feel empowered by the adults they come into daily contact with. At present there is a gulf between pupil and teacher that is not a generation thing but an authority thing.

Hero Joy, 14, Kent

〰〰

Any decisions made in the school would have to be put to the board. The board would be made up of two children, one male and one female from each class. This would mean that anything that was changed in the school would be exactly what the children would like, instead of the children not always liking what has been done.

Oliver, 12, Taunton

Power should be evenly spread throughout the school. I believe that there should be a regular council of students. A sort of governors meeting which all the school can attend and relevant issues can be voted upon. A member of the committee could then present ideas at the real governors meeting giving a valuable insight into what the students really want, rather, what it is presumed they want.

Angela, 15, Croydon

School councils and democracy are key to a happy community. Feedback should be a regular procedure ... The lower levels of articulation of younger children should demand increased explanation and all should participate in decision making for the school. And get teachers to practice empathy, this stays in the system and is the best prevention of bullying, something that every school that listens can imaginatively tackle.

Jonathan, 17, Manchester

Evidence of this passion for being heard and accompanying dissatisfaction with a system that does not listen can be found in other recently published research (Cruddas *et al.*, 2000) while support amongst 14 year-olds in England for school councils was found by Kerr to be strong, with 70 per cent of those consulted agreeing that 'electing student representatives to suggest changes in how the school is run makes schools better' (Kerr *et al.*, 2001).

Lemke (2002) ended his essay on learning by observing, 'schooling is just one, relatively recent educational arrangement' and it was an arrangement that was failing to connect with 'the complexity of the communities we live in' and to provide the skills to 'participate successfully in collaborative social activities over long time scales' (Lemke, 2002: 44). If schools are to be a successful vehicle for learning in the twenty-first century, it is essential that young people are involved in determining their nature, design, organisation, ethos and use, or even if they are needed at all. This book is about the voices of children and young people and it is only appropriate that this chapter should end as it began, with their words:

My Ideal School

School is Boring
I don't like Drama
I don't see the point in going to school
I can't be bothered coming to school
The only thing I like about going to school is PE and going to Bob [school counsellor]
I don't want to come to school
I get into trouble a lot but it doesn't bother me
My ideal school would be not coming

No learning
No strict teachers
No work
My Dad left school when he was thirteen and that's what I want to do but my Dad
and Mum want me to stay at school
I don't like listening to teachers
I would like to talk to my friends during lessons

Robert, 12, Crewe

〰〰〰

I left school last year at the age of thirteen, and enrolled at a local college to take my GCSEs. I left because I felt that the regime was oppressive and, like most oppressive regimes, coercive and difficult to change. I resented being told what to wear, what to think, what to believe, what to say and when to say it. In the average school, the children are the underclass, so low in status that they are not worth listening to.

Most discussion of the education system seems to revolve around problems of finance: class sizes, facilities, teacher recruitment etc. However, the fundamental principles on which the system is based are rarely questioned. The 'school I'd like' would be very different from the norm, mostly in its attitude to children's rights. Every effort should be made to offer accessible education, and to consult young people about what they really want from schools, in order to achieve their own aims.

Although children do not have the vote, they have to accept the law of compulsory education. They have no involvement in British democracy, nor in the running of their schools – Rules are imposed on them, and they are expected to obey, yet they have done nothing to put themselves under any obligation! One of the injustices of our education system is that school pupils have no input in the nature of their own schooling. The structure of the typical school is oligarchic, being largely controlled by the senior teachers, with some input from Governors. Yet at the same time, young people are encouraged to value justice and democracy, but not to expect it for themselves. Children, as dependants, must rely on adults to represent their interests. However, human egocentricity dictates that it is more effective for individuals to support their own rights. Adults often fail to secure important rights on children's behalf. For instance, there is no organised justice system in schools by which pupils can appeal against treatment, and exercise any power. Some suggest that school councils are a successful means of pupil representation, but I have come to the conclusion they serve only to create false consciousness. A school council has very little power, because any proposals it makes may be overruled at any stage by the supervising teacher at a meeting, or by the head teacher.

The idea of democratic schools is often ridiculed on the grounds that children lack the responsibility to govern themselves. This ignores the point that children are expected to follow rules, and so they are entitled to have their say. If applied to the adult world, the position of schoolchildren is similar to that of someone expected to obey laws made in an undemocratic society. Also, self-government may help the development of a social conscience and sense of justice in a child. Furthermore, the pupils of Summerhill are living proof that children do practise self-government effectively. More importantly, I think that, as schools are said to be microcosms of society, any truly democratic nation should extend its principles to its educational institutions.

The school I'd like would, as well as having a democratic system of justice and appeal, make its rules democratically, redistributing power, and also helping pupils to develop a sense of social justice

Lorna, 14, Ipswich

⨯⨯⨯⨯

I look around and ask myself, is this what people want?
Is this what people need? That I doubt very much.

Surrounded by greyness, panic in the bitter, dank air
People try and figure it out, asking themselves why?
Is it a fearless minority? Or a petrified majority?

I see people, content with what they have.
Happy, are these people to play along and become
A part of their system, like tin soldiers lined up
They'll take away your name, chance for a future,
But tin doesn't last, it rusts.

I'd love to come into school and hear what people really think.
Pupils have no opinion on what goes on, they just let it by.
To them, school is a place just to learn.
Surely, I hope people will only take so much,
Until they break. How long until they see?

See that it is a place to question, get the answer for yourself
Take in what the teacher has to say, then put your mark on it.
Make something individual, help yourself.

Why are they content? To fall into one category?
The Pupil, nothing else.

Is the teacher always correct? Why shouldn't you question them?
Why shouldn't they be like you?
Why shouldn't they react?
The answers are not, they aren't used to it.
Why won't anybody question them? Why? When? How?
The pupil sees the information through the teacher's eyes.

No one would consider making bread with no yeast.
It wouldn't rise. The question is,
Should we be allowed to rise?

Geraint, 15, Mold

Further reading

Alderson, P. (1995) *Listening to Children, Children Ethics and Social Research*, London: Barnardos.

Alderson, P. (2000a) *Young Children's Rights*, London: Jessica Kingsley.

Alderson, P. (2000b) 'School students' views on school councils and daily life at school', *Child and Society*, 14, 121–34.

Barnardos (1996) *Young People's Social Attitudes. Having Their Say: the Views of 12 to 19 year olds*, London: Barnados.

Birkett, D. (2001) 'The school I'd like', *Education Guardian*, 16 January, 2–4.

Butterfield, S. (1993) *Pupils' Perceptions of National Assessment: Implications for Outcomes*, London: Nuffield Education.

Christenson, P. and James, A. (2001) 'What are schools for? The temporal experience of learning', in Alanen, L. and Mayall, B. (eds) *Conceptualising Child–Adult Relationships*, London: Falmer Press.

Community Cohesion. A Report of the Independent Inquiry (Cantle) (2001), London: Home Office.

Cruddas, L., Dawn, S., Freedman, E., Pierre-MacFarlane, G. and Smith, J. (2000) *Girls' Voices. Are They on the Agenda?* London: Newhan Borough Council.

Cullingford, C. (1991) *The Inner World of the School*, London: Cassell.

Davies, J. and Brember, I. (1997) 'Did SATs lower Year 2 children's self-esteem? A four-year cross-sectional study', *Research in Education*, 57, 1–11.

Davies, J. and Brember, I. (1999) 'Reading and mathematics attainments and self-esteem in Years 2 and 6 – an eight-year cross-sectional study', *Educational Studies*, 25, 2, 145–57.

Davies, L. (1998) *School Councils and Pupil Exclusions*, Research Project Report, London: School Councils UK.

Department for Education and Employment (1999) *Social Exclusion: Pupils' Support*, London: DfEE.

Department for Education and Skills (2002) *Listening to Learn*, London: DfES.

Dewey, J. (1916) *Democracy in Education*, New York: Macmillan.

Edwards, R., Alldred, P. and David, M. (2002) 'Minding the gap. Children and young people negotiating relations between home and school', in Edwards, R. (ed.) *Children, Home and School. Regulation, Autonomy or Connection*, London: Falmer Press.

Freire, P. (1996) *Pedagogy of the Oppressed*, New York: Continuum Publishing Company.

Gore, J.M. (2001) 'Disciplining bodies: on the continuity of power relations in pedagogy', in Paechter, C., Edwards, R., Harrison, R. and Twining, P. (eds) *Learning, Space and Identity*, London: Paul Chapman Publishing.

Griffiths, R. (1998) *Educational Citizenship and Independent Learning*, London: Jessica Kingsley.

Health Education Authority (1999) *Young People and Health: the Health Behaviour of School-aged Children*, London: HEA.

Hepburn, M. (1984) 'Democratic schooling: five perspectives from research in the United States', *International Journal of Political Education*, 6, 245–62.

James, A., Jenks, C. and Prout, A. (1998) *Theorizing Childhood*, Cambridge: Polity Press.

Kerr, D., Lines, A., Blenkinsop, S. and Schagen, I. (2001) *Citizenship and Education at Age 14. A Summary of the International Findings and Preliminary Results for England*, Briefing Paper, Slough: NFER.

Klein, R. (2000) *Defying Disaffection: How Schools are Winning the Hearts and Minds of Reluctant Learners*, Stoke-on-Trent: Trentham Books.

Kushner, T. (1995) *Observing the 'Other'. Mass-Observation and 'Race'*, Mass Observation Occasional Paper No. 2, University of Sussex Library.

Lee, N. (1999) 'The challenge of childhood: the distribution of childhood's ambiguity in adult institutions', *Childhood*, 6, 4, 455–74.

Lemke, J.L. (2002) 'Becoming the village: education across lives', in Wells, G. and Claxton, G. (eds) *Learning for Life in the 21st Century*, Oxford: Blackwell.

Lord, P. and Harland, J. (2000) *Pupils' Experiences and Perspectives of the National Curriculum: Research Review*, London: Qualifications and Curriculum Authority.

Markus, T.A. (1996) 'Early nineteenth century school space and ideology', *Paedagogica Historica*, XXXI, 1, 9–50.

Matless, D. (1998) *Landscape and Englishness*, London: Reaktion Books.

Mayall, B. (2000) 'Negotiating childhoods', *Children 5–16 Research Briefing*, April, 13.

National Society for the Prevention of Cruelty to Children (1995) *A Child's View of School. Consulting Pupils to Create a Listening and Responsive School*, London: NSPCC.

Social Exclusion Unit (1998) 'Truancy and School Exclusion'. Online: available at: http://www.cabinetoffice.gov.uk/seu/index.html.

Treseder, P. (1997) *Empowering Children and Young People: A Training Manual for Promoting Involvement in Decision-Making*, London: Save the Children.

UK Implementation of the United Nations Convention on the Rights of the Child (UNCRC): An update to the UK's second report to the UN Committee on the Rights of the Child in 1999. Online: available at: http://www.cypu.gov.uk/corporate/index (accessed August 2002).

UN (1989) *Convention on the Rights of the Child*, Geneva: UN.

Walker, S. (2001) 'Consulting with children and young people', *The International Journal of Children's Rights*, 9, 1, 45–56.

Wilson, J. (1999) *Child Focused Practice*, London: Karnac Books.

Wyness, M. (2000) *Contesting Childhoods*, London: Falmer Press.

Wyness, M. (2002) 'Children, childhood and political participation: case studies of young people's councils', *The International Journal of Children's Rights*, 9, 3, 193–212.

Wyse, D. (2001) 'Felt tip pens and school councils: children's participation rights in four English schools', *Children and Society*, 15, 209–18.

Your Say (2002) Online: available at: http://www.cypu.gov.uk/consultationresults (accessed August 2002).

Part 1

Forgotten spaces

My ideal school

from birds eye view & roof taken off

Maye. Dudok de Wit
Primary: age 8

year 3,4,5&6 playground

year 3,4,5&6 playground

office

library

Sports equipment

Canteen

office

caretakers room

square ball pitch

medical room

Library

TV room

computer room

Reception

stage

Hall

Yr 1

staff mens toilet

Yr 3

Headmaster office

desk

Staff ladies toilets

Drinking room

Yr 6

Yr 4

girls toilets

boys toilets

staffroom

Yr 5

Nursery, year 1 reception & year 2 playground

store room

nursery

Nursery, year 1 reception & year 2 playground

cloak room

store room

Entrance

Chapter 1

School buildings

'A safe haven, not a prison ...'

The *Education Guardian*, when it reported the results of the competition, 'The School I'd Like' summarised the statements made by children and young people as 'The Children's Manifesto' (Birkett, *Education Guardian*, 5 June, 2002).

> The School We'd Like is:
> A beautiful school
> A comfortable school
> A safe school
> A listening school
> A flexible school
> A relevant school
> A respectful school
> A school without walls
> A school for everybody.

The school building, the landscape of the school, the spaces and places within, the décor, furnishing and features have been called 'the third teacher' (Edwards, Gandini and Forman, 1998). A beautiful, comfortable, safe and inclusive environment has, throughout the history of school architecture, generally been compromised by more pressing concerns, usually associated with cost and discipline. The material history of schooling, as conveyed in school buildings, is evident still in the villages, towns and cities of any nation. In the UK, one need not look far to locate, still functioning as schools, stone-built 'voluntary' schools of the mid-nineteenth century. The 'Board' schools of the late nineteenth century still stand, as red brick emblems of the cities in which they were built in an era which placed enormous faith in 'direct works' and 'municipalisation'. The schools built in the 1920s and 1930s reflected changes in educational policy indicating the beginning of a recognition of the diverse needs of children and consideration of health and hygiene. These decades saw the building of looser groupings of units, classrooms with larger windows and with removable walls being capable of being thrown almost entirely open. Architects worked to precise standards of lighting and ventilation as set out by the Ministry of Education. The post-war building plans saw the erection of buildings utilising modern prefabricated materials. Schools were built in large numbers, quickly and cheaply with the view that they would provide a stop gap until greater resources were available. 'Finger plan' schools, featuring one-storey classrooms set in parallel rows with a wide corridor to one side were popular. Thus started, for children, the long journey to toilets, hall and dining room as the buildings sprawled over large plots.

Already in the late 1960s, it was estimated that nearly three-quarters-of-a-million primary school children in England were being educated in schools of which the main buildings were built before 1875 (1967: Department of Education and Science 1967: 389). Standards were poor in general but there were particular problems, such as the 65 per cent of schools whose toilets were located in school playgrounds. The Plowden committee reported, 'children have to use cold, dark and sometimes even insanitary school lavatories' and remarked, 'we have heard from many sources of the dislike of school that can be created by the condition of the school lavatories' (ibid.: 391).

The new buildings erected in the 1960s and 1970s were needed to accommodate the swelling numbers on the school roll, the adoption of comprehensive secondary education and the extension of the school leaving age after 1973. Architects often used prefabricated assembly systems to help reduce costs and most new schools tended to resemble factories in their construction and style. Design aesthetics and comfort were usually given less importance than economy. However, many of the ideas about the flexible use of school buildings, first voiced by Henry Morris in the inter-war years, were revisited during this period. It was argued:

> Society is no longer prepared to make available a set of valuable buildings and resources for the exclusive use of a small, arbitrarily defined sector of the community, to be used seven hours a day for two-thirds of the year. School buildings have to be regarded therefore as a resource for the total community available to many different groups, used for many different purposes and open if necessary twenty four hours a day.
>
> (Michael Hacker of the Architects and Buildings Branch, Ministry of Education, cited in Saint, 1987: 196)

Open-plan arrangements reflecting child-centred pedagogy were criticised during the late 1970s and early 1980s. Educational policy under successive Conservative governments emphasised the importance of traditional methods of instruction and whole-class teaching rather than group collaboration and teacher facilitation. A recently concluded research study of classroom arrangements in the UK suggests, however, that for the majority, tradition overcame fashion (Comber and Wall, 2001: 100).

After decades of having to meet the enormous costs of refurbishment and repairs, the UK government in 1992 adopted the policy of financing public services including the building and refurbishment of schools via the public–private finance initiative (PFI). The first privately financed state primary school was opened in Hull in January 1999. At the time of writing, 20 public–private finance initiative contracts are already operational, a total of 30 new, rebuilt, or extensively refurbished schools are now open and another 500 are planned (the *Guardian*, 30 September 2002). However, there is some disquiet among the teaching profession about the standards and quality of buildings that have recently emerged and concern that the design of schools today will rapidly become outdated as the organisation of learning changes in the future. The UK government's own watchdog on architectural matters, the

Commission for Architecture and the Built Environment (CABE) has recently voiced concern over design standards of new schools built under the initiative. Their chief executive, Jon Rouse has stated, of the 30 PFI schools already built, many are like 'sheds without windows', and fail to comply with best-practice standards of natural light (Rouse, 2002).

CABE has warned that there is insufficient effort being made to consult the users of school buildings. 'Schools need to get involved in that process and be specific about what they need. The whole process has got to be led by the curriculum' (Fraser, CABE, *Education Guardian*, 30 September 2002). However, CABE does not advise that children and young people should be involved in the design process.

It is remarkable, in view of the fact that architectural education is very rarely provided within compulsory schooling, that there was such a wealth of material contributed to the collections in 1967 and 2001 about the shape and design of schools. However, some have argued that children are 'natural builders' or 'have a natural talent as planners and designers' (Hart, 1987; Gallagher, 1998) and that the school curriculum might be better organised to recognise this. Writing in the USA, architecture and design educator Claire Gallagher has noted, 'The typical means of instruction in our educational culture is either linguistic and/or mathematical. Rarely is any attention paid to visual or spatial thinking or problem-solving' (1998: 109). Her work with 'at risk' elementary school children in designing and planning their own neighbourhoods has illuminated how children have a distinctive knowledge and understanding of spatial environments that policy-makers rarely tap.

The 'School I'd Like' competition spontaneously produced dozens of models, hundreds of plans and thousands of implied designs of ideal sites for learning. In addition there was produced a remarkable collection of drawings and paintings through which children have expressed their ideas on curriculum, use of time, role of teachers and form of school. These design ideas address more than the shape of building and the ordering of spaces; they tell of a vision of education that reaches beyond the strict mechanics of building science.

The 1967 competition had also produced entries which were architectural in approach. Indeed, one of the winners at that time was a detailed plan produced by a 17-year-old pupil, said to want to become an architect. Like many of the plans and models contributed in 2001, this plan featured domes and pyramidal structures, circular spaces and a lot of glass.

Blishen was compelled to comment on the number of circular designs suggested by the 1967 competition entries. He noted that the young designers,

> having none of the problems of an actual architect . . . let themselves go and there can't for a very long time have been such a lavish decreeing of pleasure domes.
>
> (Blishen, 1969: 43)

He suggested that such a quantity of circular schemes were, in fact,

> reactions against a quality in school buildings that many inveigh against: their squareness. . . . Most were tired of squareness: where an actual shape was suggested, nine times out of ten it was a round one.
>
> (ibid.)

The 1967 cohort wanted schools not to resemble schools at all, but to resemble the adult world where individual privacy, comfort and relaxation were permitted. And it was not only the classrooms and building shell which were subject to the circuitous (Plate 10) but also the organisation of bodies in spaces more generally.

> There would have to be a school with rooms, but furnished with soft chairs in a circle.
>
> Richard, 15

Within a circular school with circular classrooms and spiral staircases, what becomes challenged is the institutional: the regulation and ordering of bodies in precise spaces; the processing of children as in a factory; the rehabilitation of individuals as in a prison. An alternative regularity found in nature is envisaged in schools as colonies of life and development. The outer membrane, as in a cell, is penetrable, filled with light, transparent and attracts public view (Plate 1).

Jerome Bruner has proposed that the curriculum should be conceived of as a spiral to suggest how learning is achieved through a series of ever deeper encounters 'in the processes of meaning making and our constructions of reality'. The object of instruction should not be 'coverage' but rather 'depth', and the teacher is a collaborative learner and guide to understanding which begins with an intuitive impulse, 'circling back to represent the domain more powerfully or formally as needed' (Brunner, 1996: xii). When describing the spaces for learning as 'caves' and the corridors as 'spirals', the children here could be seen to be expressing their instinctive cultural understanding of how learning occurs.

We could argue that the preference for dome-like features in the recently collected archive (see, for example, Plates 1, 3, 8, 10) can be explained simply through acknowledgement of the fact that domes are features of leisure environments that children and young people frequent. These features are representative of enjoyment, freedom, play and excitement. They are semi-permanent structures that are literally here today, gone tomorrow. They are 'light' in both senses of the word. The Millennium Dome in London had entered the consciousness of every child in Britain during the exhibition period of the year 2000, even if they had not actually visited it. And, indeed, some children did clearly state that the Dome should be turned into a school as a model from which other schools could derive inspiration.

Perhaps it could be argued, however, that we have here in this collection of material, responding to the same question over time, evidence of constancy in childhood. Traditionally the school room is square, has corners and contains rows of bodies in disciplined rank. The comments of children about the significance of this in contrast to their preferred spherical arrangements betray an understanding that a shift occurs in the organisation of authority and control in moving from the rectangular to the circular.

A recurring theme of likening school to a prison is found in competition entries, both past and present, suggesting that, from the point of view of those compelled to attend, little has altered in the basic character of school in spite of the vast extent of policy intervention over the intervening period. Blishen said of the contributions to the 1967 competition, 'When I was reading these essays, the image of the prison returned to me again and again' (1969: 14): '... we're like caged animals!' is a remark which speaks for many in the more recent collection.

Comfort, privacy, space for social activity and rest, and colourful, softly textured inviting interiors are called for by countless numbers of participants in the 2001 Archive. Once again there is continuity with the demands from the past. 'They cry out for colour, and are very conscious of the drab uniformity of many of the walls within which they sit' (Blishen, 1969: 43).

Toilets continue to be an appalling problem in many schools, over 30 years after the Plowden committee recognised the severity of the problem, and there were very few ideal schools, whether in essay, design, photographic or video format, that did not feature strongly a major criticism of the school toilets. Many suggest practical ways they can be improved but most wanted them to be less institutional, more comfortable and accessible (Plate 2). For many children, not being able to lock the toilet door safely causes distress. Local research studies support children's views. During the 1980s in Leeds, a survey was conducted of school toilets which were believed to be a breeding ground for the viruses commonly causing illness. The study found the toilets to be:

> dirty, smelly and unpleasant places which suffered from vandalism, particularly in the girls' toilets. There were broken toilet seats, no lids, insufficient supplies of toilet paper, poor hand-washing facilities and string in place of chains to flush the toilets. As a result children were unwilling to use the toilets and suffered uncomfortable afternoons as they waited until they got home to relieve their bladders and bowels.
>
> (Schweiger, 2002)

A further study in 1999 revealed that 'fifty six per cent of pupils thought their toilets were dirty, 39% did not have lockable cubicles, 41% did not have toilet paper and 29% of pupils refused to sit on the toilet seat' (Brocklebank, 2001).

Many children are still compelled to attend school buildings designed and built half-a-century ago. Distressed about the poor state of the fabric of their schools, most want more space and recognise the limitations of school design in relation to inclusive school policies. Young people in special schools who have difficulty just getting around the inadequately designed school spaces, take the opportunity to recommend change. Some argue convincingly that if the overall appearance of the school were improved then children would be more likely to want to attend and not to truant.

What emerges from the material is evidence that children have the capacity to examine critically the normal and everyday spaces in which they learn and can articulate their future in previously unimagined ways. They want to feel proud of the school to which they belong but many feel embarrassed by their surroundings. The extracts here show how clearly children regard the built environment as 'the third teacher'. To listen to these voices past and present is instructive to all educators, architects, designers and policy-makers who have responsibility for conceiving and constructing the spaces for learning which children inhabit. Seeming to understand the perspective voiced here, Paulo Freire once argued:

One of our challenges as educators is to discover what historically is possible in the sense of contributing toward the transformation of the world, giving rise to a world that is rounder, less angular, more humane.

(Freire, in Macedo, 1996: 397)

Further reading

Birkett, D. (2002) 'The Children's Manifesto', *Education Guardian*, 05.06.02: 1.

Blishen, E. (1969) *The School That I'd Like*, London: Penguin.

Brocklebank, T., Unpublished survey. *Reporter*. No. 464, March 2001: University of Leeds.

Brunner, J. (1996) *The Culture of Education*, Cambridge, MA: Harvard University Press.

CABE (2002) *Client Guide: Achieving Well Designed Schools Through PFI*. September, London: CABE.

Comber, C. and Wall, D. (2001) 'The classroom environment: a framework for learning', in Paechter, C.F., Edwards, R., Harrison, R. and Twining, P. (eds) *Learning, Space and Identity (Learning Matters)*, London: Paul Chapman Publishers.

Department of Education and Science (1967) *Children and their Primary Schools. A Report of the Central Advisory Council for Education (England). Vol. 1: The Report. (Plowden Report)*, London: HMSO.

Dudek, M. (2003) *Children's Spaces*, London: Architectural Press.

Edwards, C., Gandini, L. and Forman, G. (eds) (1998) *The Hundred Languages of Children*, 2nd edn, Greenwich, CT: Ablex.

Gallagher, C. (1998) 'The "Our Town" Project: a case for reform in urban design and classroom practice', *Emergent Paradigms in Design Education: Sustainability, Collaboration & Community*, Sydney, NSW, Australia: University of New South Wales.

Hart, R.A. (1987) 'Children's participation in planning and design. Theory, research and practice', in Weinstein, C.S. and David, T.G. (eds) *Spaces for Children. The Built Environment and Child Development*, New York: Plenum Press.

Hansen, J.M. and Childs, J. (1998) 'Creating a school where people like to be', *Educational Leadership*, 56, 1, 14–17.

Herbert, E.A. (1998) 'Design matters: how school environment affects children', *Educational Leadership*, 56, 1, 69–70.

Macedo, D. (1996) 'A dialogue: culture, language, and race', *The Harvard Educational Review*, 42, 383–98.

Paechter, C.F., Edwards, R., Harrison, R. and Twining, P. (eds) *Learning, Space and Identity (Learning Matters)*, London: Paul Chapman Publishers.

Rouse, J. (2002) (Chief Executive of CABE) Interview for the BBC *Newsnight* programme, 16.10.2002.

Saint, A. (1987) *Towards a Social Architecture. The Role of School-Building in Post-War England*, London: Yale University Press.

Seaborne, M.V.J. and Lowe, R. (1977) *The English School: Its Architecture and Organization Volume II 1870–1970*, London: Routledge & Kegan Paul.

Schweiger, M. (2002) Consultant in Communicable Disease Control, Leeds NHS Public Health Protection Unit. Unpublished survey. Online: available at: http://www.yorkshirewater.com/yorkshirewater/schools.html (accessed October 2002).

School buildings

The school I would like would be much more modern than we have now. The outside makes me sick when I come in – all the teachers cars are parked in the playground and we do not have much room to run or even play we have only a small bit even there too. . . . I would want the school to look like the city chambers, marble stairs, it is all that I want. It is just like a dream. I would love to see good people in the school. I am bad sometimes which the teachers are helping me to improve. I don't blame the teachers, it is the pupils and if this happens the school will be the best ever. Would you prefer a carpet or manky floors?

Sher, 12, Glasgow

In my perfect school there would be no square classrooms but instead, triangular shaped ones so that no one could sulk in the back row.

Sam, 14, Penryn

I would like my school to be a giant toblerone shape building with two huge 5 storey cylinders stuck to it. The 5 storey cylinders will be complete with double glazed windows. There will be lots of windows. The classrooms will be circular (so there won't be a naughty corner!) with desks that sit next to each other. The desks will have a part for your stuff. There'll be posters of star constellations on the walls. There will be hundreds and thousands of books on the wooden bookcase. There will be two doors, one leading to the playground.

Joe, 9, Clacton-on-Sea

I want lots of colours.

Liam, 4, Barnsley

**I'd like a school with buildings
that are funny shaped**
And all around the outside
Coloured cloths are draped.

Mary, primary, Newport

The school buildings should be huge cylinder like buildings and a subject on each floor; we think this is a good idea because then the teachers can't tell you to stand in the corner.

Tim and Dave, lower secondary, Oakhampton

An 'own pace room' where you can go at your own pace in English and maths and work from any text book you want. And then you can go to a marking machine where you put your work in one end and it comes out marked the other end!

Tamsin, 11, Middlesbrough

I would be delighted if I had a dream school with pretty teachers, polite children, bright colours, good displays and a pretty hall with red, blue, green, yellow, pink, brown, purple and with black, silver, gold and orange [walls] and equipment for the playground like a scooter, pretend car, rocking horses, and lots more new books and nice colours like red.

Cameron, 6, Birmingham

〰〰〰

The cloakroom is boring. We need it more colourful and it's too small so in our future school we would make it more colourful and bigger and also they should have more shelves and pegs because there is no room for our bags. We want pegs that grab your coats and bags like some hands and we want more benches, so then the cloakrooms wouldn't be a mess.

Class, ages 9 and 10, Durham

〰〰〰

I would like a bigger classroom because it is not a very big room. I would like a bigger desk in our classroom because they are very small. I would like to have our classroom painted. We would like to have swivel chairs because in our class we have small children. I would bigger room because we are all crushed. I would like to have a listening corner because when you have done all your work you can go over to the listening corner and put the headphones on but we do not have room in the class ... I would like to have a boys toilet in the class because if we did we do not need to go out of the class. I would like a Science corner because we are not quite good at Science so we can learn for our Friday test.

SB, primary, Belfast

〰〰〰

The roof of this whole building is a glass dome with parts which can be opened on hotter days. In the centre there is a fountain which can flow over a closed dome (Plate 3).

Rowan, 12, Hope Valley

〰〰〰

I really don't care if the building is old or new providing it isn't vandalised and it has its own sort of beauty. It's dispiriting to have to go every day into somewhere built as cheaply as possible and where aesthetics are thought to be the superfluous icing on the cake.

Hero Joy, 14, Kent

〰〰〰

My ideal school has a totally different setting as compared to our schools today. The school has one main compound where all classes take place and all other buildings adjoin this building. It's shape is oval ... there is an oval playground in the middle of the main compound ... The classes are all painted soft pink, sky blue, bright yellow or rich purple. The chairs in all the rooms are soft and have arms. The floors are carpeted and the carpets are cleaned during mid terms and holidays. The toilets are spacious and well equipped, with janitors that clean it regularly.

Aisha, 14, London

〰〰〰

There would also be many comfortable and informal meeting places for creative interaction in small groups on key issues, not just on the syllabus but also wider issues occurring locally and elsewhere.

Jonathan, 17, Manchester

◌◌◌◌

The basic aspects of the buildings we are taught in do not promote learning, but instead, enhance feelings of negativity. I hate waking up every weekday knowing that this day, one that is so valuable to me, will be spent in a giant magnolia prison. I want colours, I want beauty in my surroundings, but most of all I want to be filled with inspiration by a place that I can call my home from home. The colour of a room is very important; a calming sky blue for instance will make the room seem less of a cell. No person wants the fundamental years of their life spent in ugliness and why should they?

Angela, 15, Croydon

◌◌◌◌

My ideal school would be a very futuristic one. It would be made of glass and bright blue steel tubing to hold the glass in place. The ground floor of the school would be for classrooms, the outside would be painted gold and it would have many oval windows . . . The school would be very eco-friendly. On the roof there would be solar panels and wind turbines in the grounds of the school. This would enable the school to generate its own electricity. Also there would be a recycling area for all the school's paper and bottles.

Andrew, lower secondary, Bristol

◌◌◌◌

The school I would like would be in a beautiful park, with a river running by. The building would be very modern with lots of windows. Some of the windows would be made of stained glass. In the school grounds there would be a glass dome which would be warm inside and decorated with tropical plants.

Hannah, 8, Godalming

◌◌◌◌

Our school playground – it's a tiny, slanted, concrete slab which hasn't changed since Victorian times! Some teachers might say it would cost too much to extend the playground but it would definitely be worth it. You could knock down the huts in our playground and build an extra floor on top of the main school building! After all, there are about 360 of us every year and we're like caged animals!

Alun, 10, Cardiff

◌◌◌◌

The toilets are full with loads of modern technology.

• The suction bin, a bin that you place rubbish near the tube and it will suck it in.
• Smell proof doors.

All of the toilets are different colours, and have slightly different patterns on the seats. There are orange, blue and yellow tiles.

Gabriella, 10, Gloucester

◌◌◌◌

I hate walking from block to block between lessons. When it rains you get really wet. So I think we should have a dome which is glass over school which is always warm inside and never rains.

Hannah, Sara and Katie, lower secondary, Bristol

〰〰

My ideal school would look nice and bright from the outside and the teachers cars would go in a separate area where the children couldn't go. The windows would be clean and there would be no litter on the ground.

Jade, 11, Glasgow

〰〰

To help us concentrate even more
We need doors on the classroom to make sure
That noise does not disrupt us as we write
I think that this is only right.

Katie, 10, Bolton

〰〰

The kind of school I'd like would have:
Sweet smelling toilets with doors that lock.
But instead we've got:
Toilets so disgusting, they're like an old cellblock,
All grungy and mungy, only a couple that lock!

Sophie, primary, Edinburgh

〰〰

I would like to have a toilet in our class so it would be easier instead of having to walk a long way to go to the toilet.

LO, primary, Belfast

〰〰

We have the most disgusting toilets. They are small and cramped and covered in graffiti, some of which has been dated 1899. You can see over the tops of the toilets, so you don't have very much privacy. The water is a joke. It is icy cold. My dream school would have sensor taps and the soap would be refilled everyday. The cubicles would be metal and would have enough room to be able to turn around without seeing over the top. There would be air dryers in the shape of animals in the little kids toilets and twenty first century ones in the older kid's toilets. The locks on the doors are very unreliable cause you're worried you are going to get stuck in them, the locks I would like would be very easy to use and you could go to the toilet without worrying whether you were going to come out again.

My dream school would be very modern and have a very nice feel about it and everything would be very fresh.

Melissa, primary, Edinburgh

〰〰

The classrooms are round and have strawberry red walls.

Emma, 6, Oxford

〰〰

The design is based on the rebuilt courtyard at the British Museum, Tate Modern in London and also the Eden Project in Cornwall. I like this idea for a school which creates a happy, calm, working environment that inspires all young adults to learn and interact with one another in an environment that values them and treats them with respect, so they can learn to respect other people and cultures with understanding.

Alice, 13, Penryn

〜〜〜

I would like the school to have a bigger hall so you can fit more people in and you would not be crammed in. I would also like the toilets to be cleaner and have smoke alarms in them. I also would like the classrooms to have a makeover, e.g. new curtains, carpets, ceiling, chairs, tables and so on because I think you need to feel comfortable around where you are working.

Oliver, lower secondary, Reading

〜〜〜

Every classroom in our school is open to the other classrooms. Noise can be heard easily, teachers telling their class what to do and teachers telling other children off! (It's always the teachers making all the noise!). I thought about having walls fitted across the classroom, to stop all the noise.

Callum, 11, Bolton

〜〜〜

The toilets feel like you're underwater with a sound track and it is done by using the same way as a picture on the cinema, so the walls have water and sea animals. Also it is the shape of a bubble.

Arianna, 10, Bristol

〜〜〜

The basic design of our school would be very futuristic. It would be a giant glass ball and there would be an inflatable cushion on the inside to stop any break-ages. Of course it would be stuck to the ground ... there will be glass classrooms with the same design as the school.

Matthew and Joe, 9 and 10, Durham

〜〜〜

The school I would like would have to be big with lots of space. My ideal school would be just the same on the outside but with a new coat of paint and all the windows repaired ... we could have decent classrooms with nice comfortable chairs with clean desks. The classrooms could have carpets ... we could have some benches to sit down on in the playground. The thing I would like most about this new school would be the options open to us. We would be able to relax in front of your computer in maths and go down after school and have a swim. At lunchtime, if it was cold, we could go inside and watch videos or listen to music. It would be like just being at home.

Gavin, 13, Glasgow.

〜〜〜

I would like the doors of the toilets to have locks on.

Seera, 9, Richmond-upon-Thames

〜〜〜

Our school is made from a big old house,
About some things we have a grouse:
Most of us travel round in wheelchairs,
Which means we can't manage stairs.
The lift we have is very small,
It isn't big enough at all
If we could have a bigger one
We'd have more time to have some fun.
We need more room to move in class
And wider corridors so people can pass.
It really is a terrible bore
When we can't manage to open the door,
If doors would open when we shout
It would be easier to get about.

Group, ages 16–19, Bolton

ˢˢˢˢ

The Activity room will be a place to go after your work is finished. There will be several activities such as painting, an I.T. area, a reading area, a communication area, a music area and a sensory room to inspire good thoughts. The communication area is a place where you can talk to people all over the world by just putting on some headphones and a microphone . . . the machine will translate any other languages.

Sophie, 10, Swanwick

ˢˢˢˢ

My perfect school would have blue wallpaper with silver mirror stars on it and flower clocks. The feel of the wallpaper is velvet. The whole school would smell like Angel perfume. There would always be good music playing. I would not recommend rough music, for example Slim Shady.

Ellis, 7, Glasgow

ˢˢˢˢ

Art would be a huge part of the education. The children would be able to do huge murals, statues etc. to be put around the school. This will make the children feel that they made part of the school, which should hopefully reduce graffiti and vandalism.

Oliver, 12, Taunton

ˢˢˢˢ

Everybody has to use toilets in school but I think they should definitely be improved. Firstly, each toilet should have a lock on the door to make it more private. Secondly, there should be toilet paper in every cubicle. There should be full size toilets instead of tiny ones. They should be modernised and made more inviting.

Delyth, 10, Cardiff

ˢˢˢˢ

I feel very strongly about the colour of the walls of the classrooms because all the walls are white and they make you feel cold. We should have red walls because red is a nice warm colour.

Yusuf, 10, Cardiff

ˢˢˢˢ

All the students would like more space. Fiona would like wider computers so that she can see her work more easily. Jayne would like a very big hall to dance and move in. It would be nice, Zoe says, to have the doors painted red. Everyone would like a brighter, lighter school.

Zoe, Sam, Fiona, Jayne and Kirsty, Special School, Cheshire.

Chairs are really, really uncomfortable so the school should buy comfortable chairs and, if they don't do that we should be able to bring our own cushions to school. Our classrooms are disgraceful. If you don't believe us come and have a look. We would really like it if our classrooms could be painted in the pupils' choice.

Mathew and Rhys, 10, Cardiff

In the classroom, the desks would be larger and every desk would have a draw containing paper and writing materials the chairs would be leather and the back would be adjustable. There would be carpeted floors in all classrooms and many heaters.

Lindsey, 13, Glasgow

Our floor is awful. It's like a patchwork quilt full of holes. Our chair legs are always getting stuck and we're forever tripping up. Anything could be better, but we could get the floorboards sanded down and painted.

Clare, 11, Cardiff

When going to and from lessons we (all one thousand two hundred of us) have to walk down a corridor that is about one-and-a-half-year-sevens wide (which isn't very big) so we suggest wider corridors that are interesting, colourful and have art graffiti on them as we think this is what people like to gaze at as they are walking along instead of 146 pictures of some year group's trip to the middle of nowhere!

Anon, 12, Bristol

I think the school is really drab and ugly and I would like it to be nice and colourful and clean. I would like lockers to put all our books and p.e. kit in. I think the windows should be cleaned at least once a month. The blinds should be white instead of black. We should have soft chairs instead of hard chairs and nice tables and we should have nice soft carpets. There should be water coolers all around the school. The toilets are really horrible and they should be nice and clean.

Lisa, 13, Glasgow

Chapter 2

Canteens and lunchrooms
The edible landscape of school

> For all who call for schools to be more civilising settings, we need to redesign the
> forgotten spaces where informal learning occurs: schoolyards and lunchrooms
>
> (Hart, 2002)

The edible landscape of school and, in particular, the school meal, was commented
on by secondary school pupils who took part in the original 'School That I'd Like'
competition in 1967. Blishen noted how children's customary use of humour
betrayed the significance of food in their lives at school.

> If schools are ever widely improved, children will lose one of their best jokes
> and most beloved grouches. But it is clear from the evidence of these essays that
> they would endure the loss gladly. Given their attachment to the joke, there
> can't be any doubt that in a great many schools the meals are still badly cooked
> and indifferently served. The chief pleas come again and again, and are all
> represented here: not only for good cooking, but for varied menus, some say in
> the size of the meal on any particular occasion, the avoidance of banal or eccen-
> tric combinations of dishes; an opportunity to choose among alternatives; and a
> pleasant environment in which to eat.
>
> (Blishen, 1969: 149)

Every one of these pleas have been repeated a generation later, in spite of the vast
changes that have occurred in the way that food is prepared, delivered and consumed in schools (Berger, 1990).

From its inception, the edible landscape of school can be seen to have been a territory of contested desires and intentions; a battleground between the perceived
needs of the adult and the child, as well as an exhibition space for the product of
educational endeavour. One detects a sense of fear and revulsion in early accounts
of collective consumption. For example, the parliamentary committee on the
Working of the Education (School Meals) Act in 1910 noted that, in many cases,
dinner was eaten in 'a perfect pandemonium of noise' and such 'disorderly conduct'
as the throwing of food was reported. The school meal was regarded as an educational and a 'civilising process' and may 'be made to serve as a valuable object
lesson and used to reinforce the practical instruction in hygiene, cookery and
domestic economy' (Selby-Bigge, 1909: 83).

Generations of school children have experienced sitting down together at midday, usually in the school hall. This large communal space was conceived by planners of state schools as a multi-purpose facility; it was considered too costly to provide specialised lunchrooms. The specified dining area and kitchens of schools designed during the 1920s symbolised modernisation, progress and quality in state education. Partly, this was a practical necessity as schools were drawing pupils from ever larger catchment areas and returning home for the midday break was an impossibility for many (Ringshall, Miles and Kelsall, 1983).

Moreover, the school hall traditionally operates as a signifier of hierarchy, never more so than in the public school or the Oxbridge college. Collective consumption of food in large institutions is surrounded traditionally by control and authority, strictly enforced or regulated in the ordering of furniture and the arrangements of seating. Such authority and control exercised by members of staff, or by older children as monitors or prefects, is an established feature of the edible landscape of school. It was resisted in the past and is criticised once more in the collection presented here.

On a global scale, school-feeding programmes are perceived by agencies such as the World Food Programme to be the key to ending global hunger and associated inequalities. Drought and associated famine which strike areas such as Kenya immediately impact upon schools where children, especially girls, are withdrawn while their families cope with the short- or long-term crisis. UNICEF has reported a drop in school attendance of between 5 and 10 per cent in such areas at these times. Poverty, hunger or malnutrition is usually associated with the non-industrialised majority world. But the incidence of child poverty is on the increase in many Western countries and providing nutrition in the school environment is regarded as a key to tackling wider problems of inequalities and related issues.

The provision of drinks of various kinds has long been associated with state education and continues to be an issue. It was recognised early in the history of state education that the provision of free milk or warm milky drinks was an important measure to be taken against poverty and social inequalities. The provision of cocoa and malted milk drinks was a regular feature of elementary schooling between the wars, as indicated by the commercial involvement of milk drink companies. The 'Horlicks School Scheme' is one example from the inter-war period when it was claimed that the children from 6,000 schools involved were 'brighter, more alert . . . have increased energy and they are more regular in their attendance than before the introduction of the "Horlicks School Scheme"' (BBC, September 1935–June 1936). Today, the connection once established between nutrition and learning has been broken and the contributions from children and young people gathered here draw attention back to the need to recognise this essential link.

The school meal and its environment has changed considerably over two decades of deregulation and the encouragement of private contracting, but children and young people are clear in their argument that things still need to improve. This partly explains the fact that the vast majority of entries to the 2001 competition place a high importance on food and the context in which it is consumed. Some clearly enjoy their school dinners, even suggesting that they should be served twice a day, but the majority, like their predecessors a generation earlier, question the quality, quantity and value of the food they are offered and the service and atmosphere in which it is consumed.

Children seem to know that quality of food and service, together with the degree of choice, variety and time to socialise is indicative of the degree of respect afforded to them as individuals and as a group. As one girl puts it, 'adults would not put up with cold food, so why should we?' (Sarah, 9, Sheffield). Consistent is the call for more time to consume and enjoy food and drink, a more pleasant environment in which to eat and socialise and the need to be consulted as to their preferences. However, also evident in the 2001 archive are the many voices who argue that food is significant in representing and acknowledging diversity among the school community. Indeed, there is evidence of a strong recognition that respect of differences in eating habits associated with culture and belief can be a sign of a caring and inclusive school committed to tackling injustices of all kinds.

Edible landscapes are, in evolutionary terms, original landscapes. Food and drink is fundamental to survival and in the compulsory, largely controlled and increasingly scrutinised territory of the school, children past and present recognise the importance of this landscape. Its symbolic significance was recognised in the past as Blishen's children chose edible metaphors to represent nourishment of mind, body and spirit:

> Freedom to think and learn is as important to us as food, yet I am afraid that it is as scarce in our schools as food is in some parts of the world!
>
> Dermot, 17

In the ideal school:

> We will take our trip, drink milk with wise, friendly men, and go home to read.
>
> Richard, 17

In 2001, their imaginations were summoned to the possibilities of the edible landscape in the school they would like. Schools made of sweets and classrooms containing edible chairs and tables, teachers made of chocolate and blackboards made of liquorice are featured in their drawings and descriptions (Plate 4). These imaginative associations are what we might expect from young children, but they remind us that food represents fun in young minds and such images suggest a longing for school to be fun.

Water, milk or sweet drinks flow from fountains positioned as decorative and functional features in the ideal school landscape. These are sometimes dream-like and fantastic but, more often than not, entirely practical. The demand comes time and again for unrestricted access to drinking water. Carefully positioned and meticulously drawn water coolers appear in many plans of schools and classrooms. While many schools in the UK and elsewhere are experimenting with the use of water to counter dehydration and increase children's powers of concentration,[1] there is ample evidence in the 2001 archive that children know that their thirst is an educational issue (Rogers, Kainth and Smit, 2001: 57–8).

1 Yorkshire Water, 'Cool Schools'. 2,000 water coolers are being provided in all primary schools in Leeds within an associated research programme ('Cool Schools') coordinated by Yorkshire Water and St James' Hospital, Paediatric Unit.

School meals, served up in noisy halls or canteens, are associated with heaviness, dullness, grey colours and dismal moods. In both 1967 and today, children have readily associated the serving of school food with institutions such as hospitals and prisons which emphasise authority, control and the regulation of bodies. Dining areas, since they usually occupy large open spaces, are often noisy and hectic. For many children, this represents a particular area of discomfort. For a child who is feeling unwell, is simply not hungry or who needs the toilet during the meal time, the dining area can become a forbidding and threatening place. In spite of the tendency towards ever-faster consumption of food on the move, young children often crave a space of calmness within which to take time to digest their food. They want to be able to sit with their friends, not be forced to eat and have ample time to play and prepare for the afternoon lessons. This was recognised by children in the past who envisaged a school where

> we would not be thrown out at lunch time but would be allowed to go somewhere to sit and talk.
>
> Janet, 14

At the present time in the UK, school meals in primary schools are often served within an atmosphere of distrust and compulsion, sometimes within enforced silence. This goes a long way to explain the prevailing dislike of the school meals assistant or supervisor whose job it is to ensure that the meal is taken with the minimum of fuss and waste. Children's inventions of robotic dinner assistants and technological devices for avoiding contact with human beings, such as midday supervisors, betray the need for less interference and more trust.

Across time, children have recognised that the material environment reflects an attitude towards the degree of social equality recognised in dining spaces. Rather than the regular, rectilinear arrangements of bodies around tables and chairs, with the implied head of table and authoritarian regime which mirrors that found in the classroom and the rest of the school, an alternative is envisaged. What then becomes challenged is the formality and associated meanings of control in spaces which are, from the point of view of the young person, predominantly for enjoyment and social interaction. Regular or linear arrangement of furniture implies a limited choice of food and little freedom to socialise, whereas irregular arrangements and smaller groupings and circular settings implies greater choice and freedom to socialise.

There is consistency over time in the demand by children for separate and specialised eating areas, similar to those which have become expected in the adult world of work. Children and teachers today are clearly struggling in many cases to work in spaces where food is regularly consumed. Such practice might have been grudgingly tolerated during the first decades of the twentieth century. Today, with the demise of the school meal as a central plank of educational and welfare policy, the chances of listening closely to the voices of children concerning the importance of spaces for eating, drinking and socialising seem more remote than ever.

Children and young people have described here the kind of space for eating they would prefer. Having some choice over seating arrangements, whether in a large or small space, is important and better furnishing to create a warm, quieter and calmer atmosphere is called for. A preference for small-scale social eating areas within a large open space is a recurring theme. The evidence presented here is reinforced by the findings of other recent efforts to consult children about school design. 'School Works' is an organisation pioneering a programme of building improvement in creating a model refurbishment at Kingsdale School, in inner-city London. At this school, where 67 per cent of children have free school meals, it was noticed that few children actually sat down to eat, making the atmosphere rather threatening for the younger or smaller children. It could have been simply suggested that this is what young people these days prefer. However, given the chance to comment on what changes they would make to the built environment, the major concern expressed was to reduce the size of the dining space, making smaller spaces for groups to eat together. This seemed to be a universal desire since it was found that 'girls and boys did not seem to experience this differently as they all seemed to dislike the ordeal of dining at the school' (School Works, 2000).

Generations of school children and their teachers have regarded the midday meal as an ordeal to get through each day, which may explain why the memories of the school meal and the sight, smell and atmosphere of the dining hall are held by many throughout adult life. One child noted in Blishen's selection that

> School meals are ghastly affairs, which always cause disturbance among pupils and adults.
>
> Angela, 15

Contributors to the original competition commented on the oppressive and sometimes abusive atmosphere in which they were expected to take their meals.

> These systems are wrong because, particularly in boys school where senior boys have the power to beat younger boys, having power over others can give pupils an overbearing or even sadistic disposition.
>
> Alexandra, 13

Children and young people today crave to be treated with trust, and that the built learning environment might not resemble a school at all. Many have known little other than 'fast' or convenience foods and fewer families than in the past today sit down regularly around the domestic table to eat a meal. As might be expected, many children envisage the ideal school environment as featuring their favourite fast food outlets. Since the implementation of the Education Act in 1980 the Schools Meals Service has been seen as an area where cost reductions could be achieved. Local Education Authorities have been encouraged to arrange for contractors to provide meals at the most economical price. Nutritional standards which had operated since the mid-1960s were no longer of primary importance. However, the result has been a sharp deterioration in the nutritional value of food available to school pupils and pressure has been put on the government to reintroduce nutritional standards, achieved from April 2001. The argument often put today by managers of school meals contracts is that reverting to the traditional school meal would result in a total lack of uptake and the consequent haemorrhaging of the school community during lunch breaks to the local shops and cafés. But perhaps by paying more attention to the ideas for changing the edible landscape of school, and especially listening to the ideas of children and young people, this barrier to change can be removed.

In spite of major changes in the type and origins of food consumed in school there are important continuities over time which the historical perspective allows us to recognise. These continuities in children's experience and culture underline the fundamental importance of the edible school landscape for children. They draw from it in ways that allow their creative impulse to become active. Food becomes a language of communication, a shared code that children know how to interpret from their collective play. Food represents survival which goes a long way to explain why it features so strongly when children of all ages are invited to describe or design their ideal school environment. This creative outlet is important to recognise and what the historical record testifies is that, in spite of the 'McDonaldsisation' factor, the evidence shows that young children will respond to the edible landscape in creative ways while they are allowed free time together to play or socialise in the school or school yard.

Further reading

BBC, advert in *Broadcast to Schools*, September 1935–June 1936.

Berger, N. (1990) *The School Meals Service. From its Beginnings to the Present Day*, Plymouth: Northcote House Publishers

Blishen, E. (1969) *The School That I'd Like*, London: Penguin.

Buckley, M.E. (1914) *The Feeding of School Children*, London: Bell and Sons Ltd.

Burke, C. (2003) 'The edible landscape of school', in Dudek, M. (ed.) *Children's Spaces*, London: The Architectural Press.

DfES (2001) *Healthy School Lunches for Children in Primary Schools*, London: HMSO.

Hart, R. (2002) letter, 2 March, responding to article by Rothstein, R. 'Recognizing the secret value of lunchroom duty', the *New York Times*, 27 February.

Molnar, A. (1996) *Giving Kids the Business: The Commercialization of America's Schools*, Boulder, CO: Westview Press.

Ringshall, R., Miles, M. and Kelsall, F. (1983) *The Urban School. Buildings for Education in London, 1870–1980*, G.L.C. London: The Architectural Press.

Rogers, P.J., Kainth, A. and Smit, H.J. (2001) 'A drink of water can improve or impair mental performance depending on small differences in thirst', *Appetite*, 36, 57–8.

School Works (summer 2000) unpublished notes from workshops. We are grateful to School Works and the headteacher of Kingsdale School for allowing access to these notes.

Selby-Bigge, L.A. (1909) *Report on the Working of the Education (Provision of Meals) Act up to 31st March 1909.*

Canteens and lunchrooms

My head bursts with ideas that could be changed on food. Like more choices such as Indian food for the Indian children, Chinese food for the Chinese children and so on or you could just have more choices for children who wanted to try out different foods ... Sometimes I wish that lunchtimes were longer, there are times when I feel I have hardly sat down to eat and three tables have gone out to break already.

Isobel, 8, Birmingham

∽∽∾∽

I wish my school would be a flower school. I would have flower tables and chairs. I wear flower clothes. I would wear little flowers in my hair. ... I eat flower sandwiches. I drink Ribena, I have flower shaped crisps and flower shaped sweets and biscuits.

Ellie, 5, Cheshire

∽∽∾∽

The sweet school is made out of sweets
There's a pool of sweets
There's a toilet of sweets
If you go to bed there is a machine that says chewits, smarties, fruit pastels and pick
    n' mix.
If you choose a button and you get some sweets come down a curly tube.
When you work with a pen or pencil there's a sweet on the top that you can chew
    when you write.
The blackboard is liquorice. The tables are blue sweets. The children are jelly babies
    (Plate 4).

Rebecca, 8, Coventry

∽∽∾∽

This would probably be the biggest change in any school all over Britain. Instead of the often tasteless drab food provided day in day out, the school would be a given a wide range of options from countries all over the world. This would also raise cultural and racial awareness in the school and encourage the learning of languages on a wide scale.

Cerys, upper secondary, Cardiff

∽∽∾∽

I would like more time to eat my dinner. I sometimes don't finish it and I seem to get thinner.

Rachel, 9, Swanwick

∽∽∾∽

The canteen has a marble floor tiling and a domed glass roof. The tables are stainless steel long rectangles and stainless steel seats ... For food there would be a fruit bar in the morning, snacks like pastries, fruit and crisps for break. Lunch could be pasta in pesto sauces with sun dried tomatoes, chicken Caesar salad, Thai chicken curry, Chinese sweet and sour shrimp noodles, pizza, spring rolls, salads and sandwiches. The drink would be energising ice water, milkshakes, fruit juices, tea, coffee and hot chocolates. Surely young people deserve better menus than everything fried in fat or tasteless pasta with a can of sugar and chemicals.

Alice, 13, Penryn

❧❧❧

My perfect cafeteria would have see-through seats and tables and different coloured blow-up cups and plates. The food is healthy and occasionally everybody will have a chocolate bar.

Ellis, 7, Glasgow

❧❧❧

At lunch it is so extremely cramped with children, I have hardly anywhere to sit ... What happens is that I am standing around for ages just looking for space and my food is getting frozen. I say that those empty headed workmen, who build the annoying, perfect schools, should build bigger halls ... I am getting pushed around like a helpless rag doll. Sometimes my drink tips over and covers my dinner in lemonade, which makes my lovely chips, peas and beans look like goo!

Aaron, 13, Chelmsford

❧❧❧

Dinner isn't served by dinner ladies. As a matter of fact they are not served by anyone at all. They come hurtling towards us on a huge spinning wheel and it's pot luck what we get, because as soon as we decide what we want, our pick is probably on its way round again.

Jade, 9, London

❧❧❧

There would be a drinking fountain in every classroom. Because if you are dehydrated, you can't learn, it's been proved.

Megan, 13, Warminster

❧❧❧

The school I would like is a school where you can go crazy in the canteen and get out of your seats all of the time.

Kealan, 6, Derry

❧❧❧

I always dream of a classroom
Where things are cool and good,
An interactive White board
And a conveyor belt for food.

I would have computers
For every pupil there
A place to put your belongings
And a comfy leather chair

There would be a gym hall
Where you could get fit
A huge place where you can eat
And benches where you could sit

And all of the new chairs
Would even go up stairs
Because they'd be on wheels
So you could even get your meals

This is the school I'd really like
I hope you'd like it too
We'll be here at any time
Working the whole year through.

                                        Robert, 9, Durham

∽∽∽

I would have a McDonalds in my ideal school because you absolutely have to eat, and I would have a canteen for those who do not like chips etc.

                                        Lucy, 10, Lichfield

∽∽∽

Teachers and pupils should all eat together and have exactly the same food. This would probably lead to an improvement in school meals – if the teachers had to eat it too there would be lots of complaints.

                                        Nat, 11, Surbiton

∽∽∽

In the hall there will be a McDonalds in a corner, a Burger King in a corner and a KFC in a corner. In the classrooms it will be like chocolate land that means you can eat the tables and chairs. You are only allowed two pieces a lesson.

                                Amelia, upper primary, Mytholmroyd

∽∽∽

Our canteen needs decorating because at the moment it's very dull. I'd like to have new dinner ladies, because the ones we have are a bit grumpy.

Serena, 8, Wembley

∞∞∞

I love Roscoe dinners
They are very nice
My favourite choice of all
Is curry chips and rice
Sometimes we have chips
With beans or mushy peas
Lovely jacket potato
Topped with melted cheese
Pie mash and gravy
Chicken veg and chips
Make me feel so hungry
Yum yum lick my lips
On to the deserts
Jam sponge, Ice cream jelly
Washed down with juice or milk
Now I've filled my belly
How I love Roscoe School dinners
They really are the best
They take all the beating
Better than all the rest.

Liam, 9, Liverpool

∞∞∞

The food that we have to pay for at school seems 1) very expensive (about twenty-five pence a cookie and fifty pence for a tiny bottle of water!) and 2) the foods are junk food, anyway. I think that if we kept the same food we have, it should at least be made cheaper. On the other hand, if we had different food, it should be healthy and worth its price. I mean think of all the people in third world countries, who earn just fifty-seven pence a day for eight hours work … it's crazy and yet people in this country spend money on pointless food that could damage your health.

Alice, 12, Croydon

∞∞∞

The school I'd Like
Would be so fun
With no strict teachers
And in the shape of a big bun

Sarah, 11, Edinburgh

∞∞∞

Meals will be well cooked and healthy. They will be made from organic food and there will be a wide variety of vegetarian food and meals for different religious groups it will be cheap and those who can't afford it have free meals.

Isobel, 14, Ipswich

∾∾∾

For breakfast, we will have a McDonalds breakfast bar. The menu would be Egg muffin, sausages, hash browns and for drink we will have milkshake, milk and orange juice.

Anthony, 10, Romford

∾∾∾

We will have really nice school dinners, which if you have any comments or complaints about there are some forms by the till ... We will have monitors that help the dinner ladies cook. We will only have chips once a week because they are junk food. Sometimes we will have chicken nuggets, but they often cook tasty dishes with vegetables and we will eat a lot of fruit. Some of the food is grown in the garden like herbs and vegetables. We will have cookery lessons where we learn how to make cakes and biscuits and eat them for our lunch. My friend Gary once found a penny in his biscuit.

Max, 9, Birkenhead

∾∾∾

My ideal school would be on top of a volcano so it would always be warm even in the winter ... Inside there would be swimming pools, science labs, computer rooms and rooms to chill out in but most importantly, a dinner hall. But just because the dinner hall is inside, it doesn't mean that the pupils can't eat outside, maybe on the edge of the volcano! (See Plate 14)

Patrick, 10, Romford

∾∾∾

Instead of eating our dinner in our assembly hall, and having to rush our food because it is not big enough for us all, I think we should have a proper canteen for our main hot dinners and a cafeteria for snacks, drinks and to sit on rainy days and have a chat.

The cafe should be open at breaks too, so that we can get extra drinks and snacks if we need them. At the moment we have to go all afternoon without a drink, unless we save some from lunch. This is bad on hot days. This would be good for us socially, and the rooms could be used for the after school clubs as well, so the space won't ever be wasted.

Kimberley, 11, Swanwick

∾∾∾

The canteen would have several different parts, one part would be McDonalds, Burger King, Pizza Hut and a fancy restaurant which serves food from all over the world.

Aimee, 12, Glasgow

⌇⌇⌇⌇

The meals should be better and we should have an Indian cook, an Italian cook, a Chinese cook for a good variety of food.

Thomas, 11, Cardiff

⌇⌇⌇⌇

The building in the centre is the lunch room. Part of the kids' learning is having to make their own lunches. The ingredients are provided by the school but the rest is down to the children. In cooking lessons they are taught about certain foods and in the lunch time they have a chance to recreate what they have been talking about in lessons.

Amy, 13, Ipswich

⌇⌇⌇⌇

There would be a big cafeteria overlooking the river and lots of choices of healthy food. I think we should have a small farm so we can learn to plant and grow our food and look after animals. We could have a small snack bar in the grounds and take it in turns to make and sell things like bread, sandwiches and biscuits. ... We could have a special classroom in the trees to help us study nature really close up. We could have a ladder and walkway in the treetops.

Hannah, 8, Coventry

⌇⌇⌇⌇

My ideal school would be a hovercraft. There would be lots of schools, each covering a small area. The hover-school will be powered by solar power. The large roof will be made of solar panels. At night the hover school will have to land to conserve its spare energy for an early morning. When the schools land for lunch break, next to the landing site will be four small canteens, one for each year.

Katherine, 13, Ipswich

⌇⌇⌇⌇

The Hall is where we go for assembly and indoor playtime and it is used for dinnertime. We want to have a bigger hall with very soft chairs for dinnertime and spill-proof tables for if we spill anything it soaks up and if the packed lunches have forgot their pack lunches, we have some spare. We will get a robot which cooks and serves the dinner and he also clears the tables.

Class entry, 9 and 10, Durham

⌇⌇⌇⌇

At each end of the corridor there would be a nice water cooler which everyone could drink out of and ... the canteen would have to sell nice new and exciting food which is healthy, but you don't notice that it is. In the lunch break, I would enjoy a different meal from the one the day before.

Valerie, 12, Glasgow

ᔥᔥᔥ

It just isn't fair! Just because we are juniors it doesn't mean we can't have milk!!!. Why can't we have it, is it because we don't need calcium! Or are our bones strong enough already, I don't think so, or should we behave like infants to get it? Furthermore, we should have a fruit stall for when we have our break, instead of crisps and chocolate bars and what not, to help our immune system.

Bonnie Louise, 10, Cardiff

Play ground

BY TUESDAY, 6H
Armes-Mather
St. Stepen's Junior School

mming pool room

THE SCHOOL

Deep End
2m 2.5m 3m

Diving Board

m 2.5m 3m
Deep end

Chapter 3

School yards and playgrounds
'It's very big but there's nothing in it ...'

The school yard or playground where 'play time', 'break' or 'recess' happens has been described by scholars on both sides of the Atlantic as one of the 'Forgotten Spaces' of the school (Blatchford, 1989: 4; Hart, 2002). This forgetfulness is odd given the extent to which academics and others from social sciences, anthropology, folklore studies, educational and environmental psychology and, latterly, social geography have over recent years investigated the playground as a site for better understanding the nature of childhood and human development. Forgetfulness or neglect appears to underline the evidence presented here of the quite different (from children) priorities many adults have for what children 'should be doing'. Children's time in the playground is, for many teachers and other adults in schools, a source of anxiety since it is often associated in their minds with apparently chaotic and random behaviour. And certainly, as far as children are concerned, the playground is a highly significant space in the school awarding opportunities for fun and pleasure, a break from school work and most importantly, a chance to get together with friends. While, for many, it is a place of boredom, loneliness or fear, for most children, the best part of school is being with friends and trying to play as much as possible (Rousmaniere, 2001). Moreover, the playground is seldom forgotten when older people recall their school days.

The majority of entries to 'The School I'd Like' 2001 competition mention the outside environment of school, and most find it wanting. Children have stated clearly here, in their words and in their designs, that they want more space but they also want the space to be filled with things: objects, mazes, ponds, swings, gardens, slides and swimming pools. Their material visions range from tree-houses and forts, pirate ships and adventure playgrounds (presumably made from scrap materials), to full-scale theme parks with motorised rides and all the fun of the fair (Plate 5). We can observe how the concerns of younger children, for more space and equipment, compare with those of older children, for storage facilities and social spaces. It is rare that the concerns of older children are taken into account in research on play, which usually concentrates on the experience of the younger child (Blatchford, 1996: 62–3). Therefore, we have a unique opportunity here to view this important space from across the school age-range.

Certain themes emerge, the strongest among the younger children being a need for more equipment and objects to play with: swings and climbing apparatus are the most popular. However, while children are certainly concerned with meeting their own needs, there is evidence, expressed through a desire for the school grounds to cater for a variety of activities, of consideration for others of different ages and different temperaments. Related to this is a concern for comfort and safety: school yards are in the main colourless, hard spaces and children feel their own vulnerability and that of others in such an environment. Colourless, empty school yards surrounding the outside of a school are what the outside world sees first of a school and children express a concern here that this greyness reflects upon themselves and the way that the school regards them. This awareness has been noted by others in research carried out under the Learning Through Landscapes initiative.

> The appearance of school grounds was also symbolic for children of the way the school valued them – a reflection of self. Because most children believed the grounds had been created – 'put there' – for them, if the place was 'ugly' or 'boring' or 'gross', this was read by the children as a reflection of the way the school felt about them.
>
> (Titman, 1994: 84)

A further theme expressed by younger children and adolescents is the need for more natural features: water, wildlife and animals are commonly called for.

The playground did not feature as an important section of the collection of material edited by Blishen. This is partly explained by the age group of the participants in the original competition: all were in secondary education. However, there has emerged over the past 30 years, starting with the adventure playground movement of the 1970s (Bengtsson, 1972), an increase of scholarly interest and research in the importance of play and spaces for play in childhood, an interest which was in its infancy in the late 1960s. Continuous with the past are expressed needs for a greener, more interesting environment. One of Blishen's children commented that the school yard was

> like the aftermath of a hurricane in which are left bald patches of grass, a few scrubby bushes and one or two wind-blasted roses. It does not seem to be the done thing to have trees around.
>
> Jane, 15

Then, as now, variety was considered to be essential:

> I like plenty of space to play in at the breaks, with a variation of grass, concrete, trees and bushes.
>
> Janet, 13

While it has been argued that the playground has been one of the main settings for outside play completely free from adult control (Blatchford, Creeser and Mooney, 1990: 163–74), this patch of ground of varying shape and size has, in fact, been a territory of adult intervention from the early years of state education. The 'uncovered school room' as the school playground was described in the nineteenth century, was considered to be a space of considerable importance in the shaping of children's bodies and the moulding of their minds. As early as 1821, Samuel Wilderspin (1792–1866) installed infant playgrounds in his schools designed according to his beliefs in active learning containing flower beds, trees and 'circular swings', as well as being more spacious than the playgrounds for older children. Swings, parallel bars and covered areas were considered to be ideal in school playgrounds of the 1860s and 1870s (Bennellick, in Adams, 1990: 80). Though, increasingly, open space was designed for marching and drilling purposes, it was felt that yards should 'always be supplied with the proper appliances for play' (Robson, 1877: 192). Indeed, playground apparatus was considered as important as classroom furniture. At that time, the adult 'neglect' of play time in school yards was commented upon. Already becoming a 'forgotten space', teachers and school managers were reported to dislike the trouble of overseeing outside play activities despite the evidence of its importance in schooling (ibid.: 191) and its role in enabling children to express their feelings about schooling, a tradition which continues to this day (Pellegrini and Blatchford, 2000: 57–77). It was noted that:

> a spirit of lawlessness often reigns supreme in the playground, slates, windows and other property become continually damaged and the more timid children are kept in a state of terror.
>
> (Robson, 1877: 192)

However, few teachers took the advice offered by Edward Robson, architect to the School Board for London, and most viewed the yard surrounding the school as the site for physical exercise, and so it became established as an empty, colourless space characterised by the adult control of young bodies. When pavilions were erected, covering part of the yard, these were intended to protect children from the elements when exercising rather than to encourage free play (Robson, 1877: 191).

The early concern for the training and discipline of the body became supplanted with a concern for health and hygiene during the 1930s and, as the concept of physical education developed, school grounds became more associated with sports activities which led to an emphasis on the provision of playing surfaces and fields. Any equipment that had been provided was considered to be more useful indoors in the gymnasium. However, for the very young child in nursery and infant schools, the playground was considered to be important for learning, eating, sleeping and playing. 'It should be full of suggestions, places to explore, mounds and hollows and steps and tress' (Myles Wright and Gardner-Medwin, 1938: 23). Jungle-gyms, flower and vegetable gardens, pets and plenty of water were thought of as essential in planning school environments for the youngest children. For older children, it was thought that 'well arranged drinking fountains, seats, flower borders and games equipment shed can do much to avoid a desolate appearance' (ibid.: 50). However, for most of the past century, the notion of exercise and learning has overlaid the concept of play or enjoyment and the ideas of the past have been supplanted by ever more emphasis on academic achievement inside the school building (Adams, 1990: 81).

Since the 1960s, a research literature has emerged following the pioneering work of Iona and Peter Opie who, during the 1950s, recorded the richness of playground games and activities in the United Kingdom (Opie and Opie, 1959, 1969). The focus of much of this research interest has been concerned with discipline and indiscipline in the playground, particularly in relation to widespread concerns about bullying (Blatchford, 1989); learning, health and socialisation (Sutton-Smith, 1998;

Blatchford, 1999; Pellegrini and Blatchford, 2000). More recently, two major factors have been considered as significantly impacting on children's break time in the United Kingdom: the increasing constraints on time brought about by the introduction of the National Curriculum; and the increased awareness in schools of the possibilities of litigation. Peter Blatchford has, in recent work, referred to 'concerns about children's safety which have led to the dismantling of some older playground apparatus' (Blatchford, 1998: 6).

Elementary schools in the United States, Canada and Australia have a stronger tradition of providing play equipment than is the case in the United Kingdom, where it has been very rare indeed. Only for a short time during the late 1960s and early 1970s, when the value of play came to the forefront of the educational arena, did educationalists and school architects equip some playgrounds with play apparatus such as climbing frames and walls, sand and water (Thomson, 2002). Swings, climbing frames and other apparatus are standard in some Scandinavian countries such as Iceland. However, there is a tendency towards the dismantling of such equipment where society is becoming more litigious. In Australia, contemporary school playground concerns are 'rooted in fears about playground safety because of poorly designed and substandard playground equipment' and the 'legal ramifications' of playground injuries due to poorly maintained equipment. Primary schools in Australia had, by the early 1990s, 'removed most of their playground equipment, particularly the moving apparatus such as swings, seesaws and roundabouts (Evans, 1990: 212).

It is well recognised that the types of play children engage in changes radically when they move from their primary or elementary school to their secondary or high school (Pellegrini and Blatchford, 2000: 63–5). Many ethnographic studies have uncovered a richness in the imaginative and creative play that survives in school playgrounds which challenges the widely held belief that childhood has changed so much that 'they don't know how to play anymore' (Thomson, 2001: 7). This 'separate, child-governed break time culture' is important to recognise since it appears to operate independently given the basic requirements of time and space. However, the evidence is clear from the extracts assembled here that children are also caught up in a wider cultural understanding of play; one which regards children as a key area of the leisure industries market.

One of the major changes affecting childhood experience over the past 30 years has been the growth of the leisure and entertainment industries and associated privatisation of public spaces for play. A recent consultation exercise carried out by the UK government Children and Young People's Unit showed that improved leisure facilities were number one in the list of needs expressed by young people aged 13 to 19 (Children and Young People's Unit, 2002). It would be odd if this change were not reflected in commentary by children in what is one of the last spaces for outdoor play left to them. We can see the impact of children's experience of leisure theme parks in the images and texts that form an important part of their ideas for school playgrounds. How should we interpret this since it seems to lead in an entirely different direction from the major concerns of ethnographers who emphasise how young children tend to shun such formal playground provision in favour of creative and imaginative play?

Children and young people view the playground from the point of view of having fun. For the majority, the ultimate feature would be a swimming pool. A 'cool' school with 'swimming pool' was one of the most common rhymes presented. From their point of view, why shouldn't a school yard resemble the best playground they have ever visited? And today, more often than not, several children in school will have visited one of the many Disneyland theme parks or similar spaces. For children, the object is not learning, even though they may well learn. From their perspective the playground is for play and adventure. Their thoughts are coloured by larger than life theme park excesses and their plans seem to be totally at odds with the increasingly restricted time that schools are allowing children to play freely (Pellegrini and Blatchford, 2000: 69–72).

If we are to follow Blatchford's advice in 'taking pupils seriously' (Blatchford, 1996), we need to allow them to help shape the agenda for school improvement which includes, as a priority for children, space and time for play. This can encourage the adult world to recognise that children are children and must play. Their involvement in any process of change in the landscape of school is crucial if 'improvements' are to have meaning for children, lasting effect in the well-being of a school and long-term impact on the health of young citizenry.

Further reading

Adams, E. (1990) *Learning Through Landscapes. A Report on the Use, Design, Management and Development of School Grounds*, Winchester: Learning Through Landscapes Trust.

Bengtsson, A. (1972) *Adventure Playgrounds*, New York, NY: Praeger.

Blatchford, P. (1989) *Playtime in the Primary School: Problems and Improvements*, London: NFER-Nelson.

Blatchford, P. (1996) 'Taking pupils seriously. Recent research and initiatives on breaktime in schools', *Education 3–13*, October.

Blatchford, P. (1998) *Social Life in Schools. Pupils' Experience of Breaktime and Seven to Sixteen Years*, London: Falmer.

Blatchford, P., Creeser, R. and Mooney, A. (1990) 'Playgrounds games and playtime: the children's view', *Educational Research*, 32, 3, 163–74.

Blishen, E. (1969) *The School That I'd Like*, London: Penguin.

Children and Young People's Unit, UK government (2002) Consultation Report. Online: available at: http://www.cypu.gov.uk/.

Evans, J. (1990) 'The teacher role in playground supervision', *Play and Culture*, 3, 219–34.

Hart, R.A. (1987) 'Children's participation in planning and design. Theory, research and practice', in Weinstein, C.S. and David, T.G. (eds) *Spaces for Children. The Built Environment and Child Development*, New York, NY: Plenum Press.

Hart, R.A. (2002) letter, the *New York Times*, 2 March.

Lucas, W. (1994) 'The power of school grounds: the philosophy and practice of learning through landscapes', in Blatchford, P. and Sharp, S. (eds) *Breaktime and the School: Understanding and Changing Playground Behaviour*, London: Routledge.

Myles Wright, H. and Gardner-Medwin, R. (1938) *The Design of Nursery and Elementary Schools*, London: The Architectural Press.

Opie, I. and P. (1959) *The Lore and Language of Schoolchildren*, Oxford: Oxford University Press.

Opie, I. and P. (1969) *Children's Games in Street and Playground*, Oxford: Oxford University Press.

Pellegrini, A.D. and Blatchford, P. (2000) *The Child at School*, London: Arnold.

Robson, E.R. (1877) *School Architecture. Practical Remarks on the Planning, Designing, Building and Furnishing of School-Houses*, London: John Murray.

Rousmaniere, K. (2001) 'Questioning the visual in the history of education', *History of Education*, 30, 2, 109–16.

Sutton-Smith, B. (1998) *The Ambiguity of Play*, Cambridge, MA: Harvard University Press.

Thomson, S. (2002) 'Playground or playpound: the contested terrain of the primary school playground'. Paper presented at the 'Dimensions of Play' conference, National Centre for English Cultural Tradition, University of Sheffield, 24–27 July.

Titman, W. (1994) *Special Places; Special People. The Hidden Curriculum of School Grounds*, Godlaming: World Wide Fund for Nature/Learning Through Landscapes.

School yards and playgrounds

... the school yard.
I would like a big school with big open fields.
Where I could run around and let off some steam.
Instead of sitting in classes doing maths and spelling words
I could work outside and listen to the birds
No more shouting from my teacher
Just the lovely sounds of nature.

Conor, 7, Coventry

∞∞∞

We did brainstorming and we got 45 ideas for the playground. Playtimes are going to be better with all our ideas and just more things to do. We'd like toys like in a park with swings, slides, snakes and ladders and a climbing frame, a maze with flowers surrounding it. Swings is the most popular for everyone, then boys want football and girls want a quiet place and swings as well. Grown ups want the quiet place and a swing. Some little ones want a dinosaur.

More play areas and marking hopscotch, more space for the kids to run about in. Girls like skipping more than boys so they need some space for skipping and a good rope. We like playing basketball but we haven't got proper nets so we'd like some of those. Lots of people want picnic tables and benches for the playground and a private space to talk about things with your friends and a shelter from wind, sun and rain so they won't get wet. Some people don't like running about or playing football and things. If someone is feeling poorly or upset they want to be alone or quiet with their friends.

Gary and Nathan, 14 and 15, Huddersfield

∞∞∞

The playground is boring in our school because there's nothing to play with.
I want a playhouse in the playground and a hopscotch. I would like to see the flowers grow. I would like the building bright colours and painted it will look nice. I don't like to be lonely. It would be nice if there was a pond and some frogs inside the pond and some tadpoles. It will look nice if there were rainbows on the side of the classroom and the ceiling painted blue. If there was a flower garden it will look beautiful and wonderful and gorgeous. If there was new apparatus people would be nice to each other.

Sebiah, 6, Coventry

∞∞∞

There would be more effort to look after the environment. There would be a different litter picking group which would go out at lunchtime every day.

Rachel, 14, Shipley

⌇⌇⌇⌇

Outside, there is a football pitch, a basketball court and tennis courts. There is a playground with slides, swings and roundabouts. There is an in-door wonder garden with coke and lemonade fountains and benches made of unmeltable chocolate. Plants are made of pizza, pasta and sweets.

Carmen, 12, Sheffield

⌇⌇⌇⌇

We need signs for visitors to see where they are going. Bird boxes so that you can see the birds in the drive when you're walking. More flowers for the drive to smell nice and look nice. More lights so you can see where you're going at night.

Gary, 14, Huddersfield

⌇⌇⌇⌇

More play time and a play area for the little ones and they can come out and see the older ones. Also, each child can have a buddy. There will be a private space for misbehaved children ... a remote control car track, a roller blade track with some tunnels. A children's garden to learn how to garden. There will also be an adventure playground because children like adventures.

Marikka, 8, Leeds

⌇⌇⌇⌇

The other night, I had a dream. I had a dream that the boring, dull, school days were over ... I walked to school, and was greeted by the welcome sign on the fluorescent green gates. I walked down the yellow path that led to the school buildings that surrounded the big playground. Each building was painted a different colour. At break time there were lots of activities that students did so they were never left bored. ... There was a big sports arena. There was a football pitch, a basketball court, badminton court, rounders/baseball pitch and tennis court. They all had floodlights and the arena had an electric roof which you could open right up and it was like you were outside, so that in summer you wouldn't get hot and bothered. There was also a swimming pool building, which was made of glass and had an electric roof as well.

Mike, 15, London

⌇⌇⌇⌇

In the playground, I would like to have grass ... and climbing frames, swings and slides and more important there should be different spaces for different things like sports or activities. ... I would also like to have trees because on the hot days we would be able to relax on the benches under the trees.

Ellerie, 10, Cardiff

⌇⌇⌇⌇

A playground just like Alton Towers
Where we can play for hours and hours

Class, 5 and 6, Birmingham

⌇⌇⌇⌇

Ideally, there will be a lawn on the outside so when one looks out of the window, there is neat and tidy greenery. Green soothes and clears the mind allowing one to focus on the learning.

Jatinkumar, 13, London

❀❀❀

Nowadays in school you have a small selection of clubs but in a dream school there would be a vast selection of things such as doing a spot of gardening in the east courtyard which is at the back of school and has 14 beautiful peacocks running around in it not frightened at all by the children's approaches!

Alice and Prema, 8, Birmingham

❀❀❀

Outside the school there would be a bike shed with a roof so those pupils who ride to school can keep their bikes dry. The shed would be locked during the day so that bikes cannot be vandalized.

Matthew, 13, Penryn

❀❀❀

The school I dream of has a wildlife garden, a wood as well as a fantastic adventure playground with a wooden pirate ship big enough to climb on.

Alix, 7, Oxford

❀❀❀

The playground should be made of a spongy tarmac so that when we fall over we don't hurt ourselves.

Especially for those who haven't got pets in my Dream School there would be animals such as rabbits, hamsters, goats, perhaps a pig or two and some cows and sheep and any animals that a child may want. The children would take it in turns to feed, clean and look after the animals, playing with them at break times.

In my Dream School as another outside play area I think we should have a jungle play area. In here there would be big nets with big squares which hang from wooden poles that rocks in the wind and ropes to swing from pole to pole. And here would be balancing poles and rope bridges for us to swing along and slides with trees made into steps and a metal slide at the top and perhaps a curving slide around a tree.

There should be a short football pitch with goal posts and there should be basket-ball areas.

I would like a quiet corner where we could sit and read or talk in nice days with soft benches to sit on and tables with umbrellas over them when it is a sunny day.

Andrew, 11, Birmingham

❀❀❀

I would like to change our school playground. It's very big but there's nothing in it. What I would like in my school playground is a football pitch with grass. (We've already got a football pitch but there's no grass.) We would like some swings and slides in our playground and a climbing frame. There needs to be colour in our playground because our walls are just plain bricks.

LMcC, 11, Belfast

❀❀❀

The school I'd like would not be a perfect one but one in perfect surroundings. There would be no concrete but instead, grass. There would be a restful garden with benches and flower beds. It would be a place for those who want a quiet moment for thought to go and sit. It would also have a place to sit in in the winter.

Elizabeth, upper secondary, Suffolk

My playground will have some swings that have the safety black pavement under them. It will also have a huge rectangle in the middle of the playground filled with bark for a slide, climbing frame, monkey bars and all other great play activities.

My dream school field will have two football pitches and a forest for when you want a relaxing walk or sit down. It will have some lovely colourful flowers, which also have quite a nice smell.

It will also have a huge pond with pretty flowers round the edge. It will have lots of frogs, tadpoles and a few fish. Any person who goes to visit the pond would have to be very quiet and there would not be cruelty to the animals.

Emilee-Chyna, 10, Clacton-on-Sea

The type of school I would design would be light and airy with solar panels on the roof to provide heating and hot water. There would be patio doors in each classroom opening on to a large courtyard, with a glass covered way all around so the children could still go out when it rained, big enough to play under with tables and chairs so that it could be used as a picnic area in the summer. A large playground would be in the centre with lots of games and things to do at lunchtime. Through a small walkway would be a large patch of grass so that ball games could be played there with tall trees and a nature garden ... Inside the school there would be two teachers in each classroom so that the children would get more attention.

Emma, primary, Reading

The playground has lots of trees we can shelter under when it's hot. There is a big tree house with rope ladders to get in and ivy growing all around it which camouflages it. It is a great place for hiding in and playing gangsters. Sometimes the teacher on playground duty joins in or sits at the top and watches all the other children. In the summer, when the grass is really long, instead of using a tractor to cut it, we bring some horses from the farm and pen them in. Then when the grass is short, we can have a ride on the horses and help the farmer clear away the manure. In the winter it is so muddy you could think it was rice field and we devise ways of draining away the water. Each child also has their own bit of garden around the field and we grow vegetables and flowers.

Max, 9, Birkenhead

The fields house animals such as sheep goats and pigs ... the grounds also have fruit trees and vegetables that can be used for school dinners ... there is a recycling centre that is attached to the school by a tube. This centre recycles things like paper and pencil sharpenings (Plate 6).

Ben, 10, Sutton

Part 2

Learning and knowing

Indoors

(miniture version)

What Woodbreak School Looks Like??

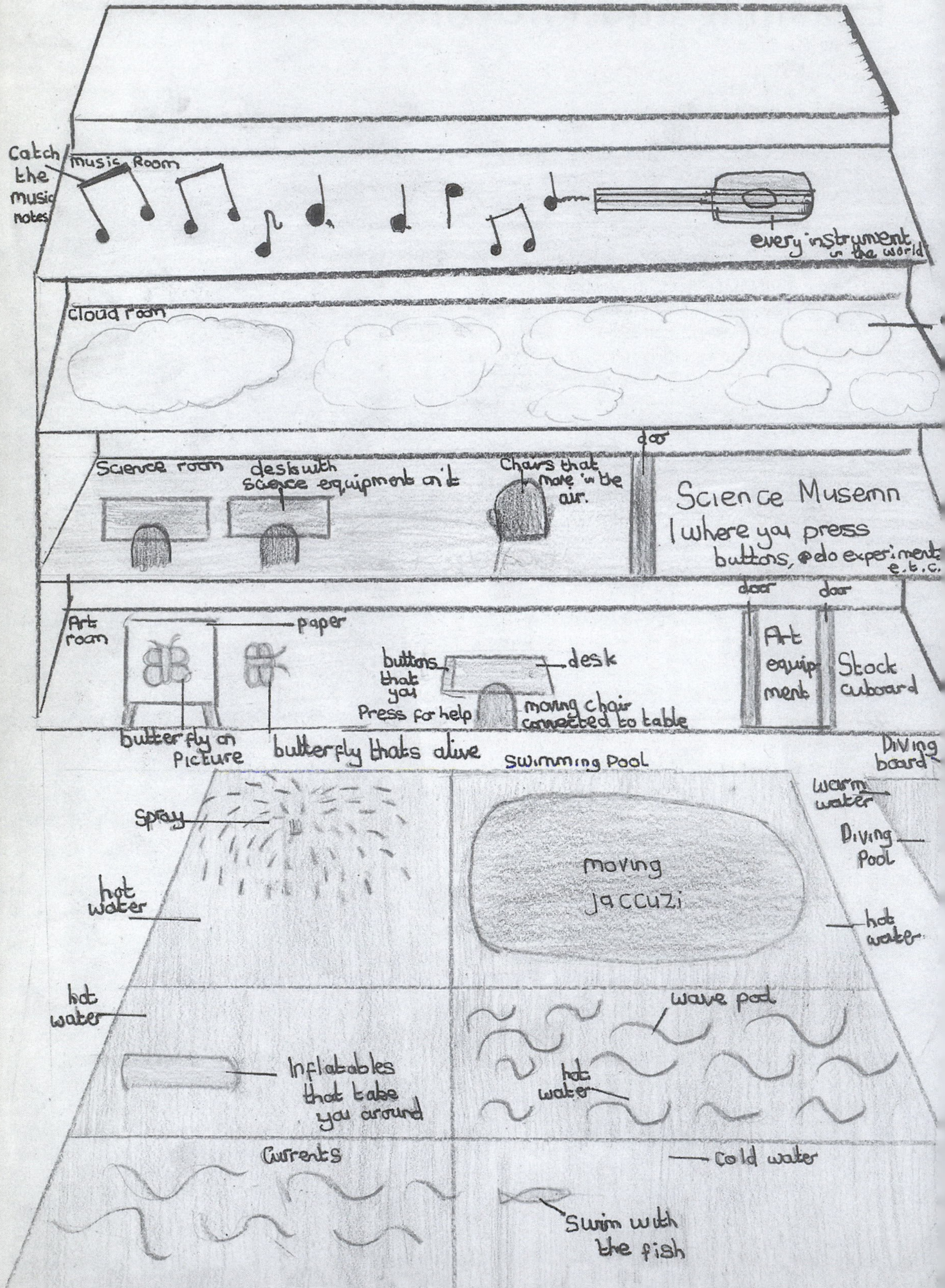

Chapter 4

Knowledge and the curriculum

'The notion of writing prize-winning essays on tropical rainforests without taking some action would be seen as strange'

> Is life divided up into sections? No, I say.
> Then why have subjects at school?
> Teach living at school,
> And living means understanding,
> And understanding is all.
>
> (Blishen, 1969: 10)

In 1967, young people questioned the subdivision of knowledge in the curriculum of schools where 'everything learnt is second hand'. As Blishen noted:

> they want excitement; they want a form of learning for which the word, for so many of them, is 'research'; they want to discover how to be responsible for themselves and their own ideas. They want simply to discover.
>
> (ibid.: 7)

At that time, the voices of school pupils seemed to chime with contemporary educational research and commentary. During the same year that the initial 'School I'd Like' competition had been held, the Plowden Committee report 'Children and Their Primary Schools' was published, arguing strongly for children to be directors of their own learning. Teacher and writer, John Holt (1967), had published his critique of teaching and learning in the primary school. The learning theories of Vygotsky, which talked of harnessing the child's natural curiosity and facilitating learning rather than teaching facts, were slowly, through translation, becoming known. The popularisation of such theories in the west was the result of the pioneering research and translation activity of the historian of education, Brian Simon, and his wife, Joan (Simon, 1998: 82). Although Blishen could not find in the secondary school entries he edited any indication of greater flexibility and openness in the organisation of the curriculum, there was a sense that a great turn around in educational practice was on the horizon.

Such optimism was expressed clearly by youngsters at the time:

> In the future the school will try to present material so that the student will become deeply involved and interested in his work; for the student who enjoys his work is always the one who makes good progress and understands his work as opposed to

simply learning it. To this end there would be no such things as set 'lessons' and boundaries between subjects would be freely crossed.

K. (boy), 17

A generation on, it could be argued that the organisation of learning has never before been so rigidly organised and that subject boundaries have never been more strictly observed. Today's children are acutely aware of this and suspect that such rigidity is not beneficial to them or to society. Barriers, borders and the structural rigidity of the school system once again come under criticism. They describe new forms of organising knowledge around interdisciplinary thematic terrains or dimensions. Questioning the division of learners according to age and ability and the division of teachers according to specialism, they call for a curriculum driven by curiosity, adventure and collective endeavour. They want to learn in response to a need to know and understand, both for themselves and for their communities and the wider world. Knowledge and skills acquired in school should be immediately useful and applied, thus reinforcing learning and contributing to society. Schooling for efficiency should be replaced by education for fulfilment.

Children and young people perceive the curriculum in schools to be too limited and inflexible, restricting their chances of drawing effectively from knowledge and skills later in life. They appear impatient and eager to explore and contribute to all of human knowledge and experience, rather than to simply receive the dry, sterile, subject-driven version presented to them. They would appear to agree with Ted Wragg, Professor of Education at the University of Exeter who has argued that, 'Classrooms should be creative and dynamic places, not graveyards of dry prescription' (Wragg, the *Guardian Education Supplement*, 16 April 2002) and they would seem to support the premise of mathematician and philosopher A.N. Whitehead who, at the beginning of the twentieth century observed: 'For successful education there must always be certain freshness in the knowledge dealt with ... Knowledge does not keep any better than fish' (Whitehead, 1929: 147).

Creativity is an essential dynamic in childhood and yet most authorities would accept it requires space, time and stimulation to flourish (Edwards, Gandini and Foreman, 1998; Robinson Report, 1999; Craft, 2000). Official recognition has been given to the vital importance of enhancing creativity through the curriculum in language which speaks to the concerns of children voiced in the 2001 archive:

> The curriculum should enable pupils to think creatively and critically, to solve problems and make a difference for the better. It should give them the opportunity to be creative, innovative, enterprising and capable of leadership to equip them for their future lives as workers and citizens.
>
> (QCA, 1999: 11)

Others have reminded us of the importance of recognising the right of children to determine the creative element in their learning: 'they are the best evaluators and most sensitive judges of the values and usefulness of creativity' (Malaguzzi, 1993: 75).

Unlike their elders, children seem unconvinced that an academic curriculum relying on the latest technologies will equip them sufficiently for life in the twenty-first century. They view themselves as global citizens whose futures might lie in any part of the globe. Metaphors of planetary exploration betray a curiosity and consciousness about the enormity and complexity of human experience and knowledge (Plate 7). The pupils are aware, to a far greater extent than previous generations, of the diversity of peoples, their cultures and the richness and depth of their histories; the ideas presented here reflect an eagerness to dig deep, to meet challenges, to explore and survive. But like the voices of children before them, children today recognise that their learning is restricted by barriers set up against their accessing fields of knowledge held by policy-makers to be inappropriate for their age.

In 1978, Her Majesty's Inspectors (HMI), having conducted a detailed survey of teaching and standards in 540 primary schools, concluded:

> The general educational progress of children and their competence in the basic skills appear to have benefited where they were involved in a programme of work that included art and craft, history and geography, music and physical education, and science, as well as language, mathematics, religious and moral education ...
>
> (HMI, 1978; cited in OFSTED, 2002: 1)

Primary school children have argued here that they should be given the opportunity to make sense of the world they inhabit through gaining access to a broader curriculum 'to expand pupil's knowledge of world politics and world affairs'. The UK Office for Standards in Education (OFSTED) appears to agree, concluding in its report on the curriculum in 'successful' primary schools in October 2002 that the implementation of the literacy and numeracy strategies had led to 'problems of coverage ... particularly marked in design and technology, art, music, geography and religious education' (OFSTED, 2002: 3). The evidence given by primary school age children in the 'School I'd Like' archive is testimony to this fact. And pupils in secondary education are still waiting for the vision offered by this 17 year old in 1967:

> Give me the school where, as from the age of thirteen to fourteen plus, we will have the chance to learn and discuss elementary philosophy, psychology, logic, contemporary world affairs, economics, arts.
>
> Cosette, 17

The need for specialisation is recognised in the writings of young people past and present but they regard as more important the need to build a foundation which is characterised by a holistic emphasis in teaching and learning. Looking around them, they recognise and can evaluate the consequences of becoming specialised in highly restricted areas of knowledge. They question the divisions set up between the arts and sciences, the rural and the urban. They point out the disadvantages of society's valuing more highly certain skills over others. In so doing, their perspective betrays their sense of a highly volatile and fluid world; a place where knowledge and understanding grounded in limited contemporary certainties might, over night, become irrelevant. They argue that pupils and teachers should be furnished with such wisdom and knowledge that they are equipped to survive not just in the market place but in the global village.

Jerome Bruner has described the subject closest to life as it is lived as 'the human Past, Present and Possible', generally referred to in schools as social studies, history and literature. He has called for more passion and courage in the pursuit of knowledge in this area. The approach to learning must, he argues, incorporate the ideas of agency: taking more control of our own mental activity; reflection: making learning make sense; collaboration: sharing the resources of the mix of human beings involved in teaching and learning; and culture; the way of life and thought that we construct (Bruner, 1996). These ideas are clearly reflected by the children and young people below who cry out for relevancy and agency in their intimate relationship with knowledge.

In contrast to the 1960s, the government today expects an ever increasing proportion of youngsters to continue in full-time education until their eighteenth birthday and the cusp of adulthood. This imposed delay in taking a full part in society is reflected here. Rather than a place where facts are learned and possibly even discussed, children and young people recognise the potential for the school community to become itself an agent of change and betterment rather than a place where teachers and learners are restricted in their powers. There is resistance to such a vision of the school not just in the United Kingdom. The educational critic, Henri Giroux, has remarked on the USA experience:

> any attempt to transform the nation's classrooms into places where future citizens learn to critically engage politics and received knowledge both inside and outside the classroom are perceived as either irrelevant or unprofessional.
>
> (Giroux, 2000: 4)

Yet, it appears from the evidence collected here that the relevance of such critical engagement is undisputed and children are tired of waiting in the wings for their opportunity to challenge and change the world.

Further reading

Blishen, E. (1969) *The School That I'd Like*, London: Penguin.

Brunner, J. (1996) *The Culture of Education*, Cambridge, MA: Harvard University Press.

Craft, A. (2000) *Creativity Across the Primary Curriculum. Framing and Developing Practice*, London: Routledge.

Edwards, Carolyn P., Gandini, Lella and Forman, George (eds) (1998) *The Hundred Languages of Children: the Reggio Emilia Approach to Early Childhood Education – Advanced Reflections*, Norwood, NJ: Ablex.

Giroux, H.A. (2000) *Stealing Innocence: Youth, Corporate Power and the Politics of Culture*, New York, NY: Palgave Macmillan.

Holt, J. (1967) *How Children Learn*, London: Penguin.

Holt, J. (1970) *The Underachieving School*, London: Pitman.

Malaguzzi, L. (1993) 'History, ideas and basic philosophy: an interview with Lella Gandini', in Edwards, Carolyn P., Gandini, Lella and Forman, George (eds) (1998) *The Hundred Languages of Children: the Reggio Emilia Approach to Early Childhood Education – Advanced Reflections*, Norwood, NJ: Ablex.

Morris, K. (2000) 'Can children do philosophy?', *Journal of Philosophy of Education*, 34, 2, 261–79.

Office for Standards in Education (OFSTED) (2002) *The Curriculum in Successful Primary Schools*, HMI 553, October.

Peacock, A. (2000) 'What education do you miss by going to school? Children's 'coming-to-knowing' about science and their environment', *Interchange*, 31, 2/3, 197–210.

Qualifications and Curriculum Authority (QCA) (1999) *The National Curriculum: Handbook for Primary Teachers in England Key Stages 1 and 2*, London: DfEE and QCA.

Robinson Report, Department for Culture, Media and Sport. National Advisory Committee on Creative and Cultural Education (1999) *All our Futures: Creativity, Culture and Education*, London: DfEE.

Simon, B. (1998) *A Life in Education*, London: Lawrence and Wishart.

Whitehead, A.N. (1929) *The Aims of Education and Other Essays*, New York, NY: Macmillan.

Wragg, E. (2002) *Wise Words*. Online: available at: http://education.guardian.co.uk/Print/0,3858,4394246,00.html (accessed February 2003).

Knowledge and the curriculum

At present, I feel that there is a very limited curriculum, which I believe to be bad for society. I believe that changing a tyre or mending a tear in a sweater should be equally as important as Maths or Science.

Also, I believe that the curriculum should contain the need for experiences, such as going to the beach, the countryside, a table-tennis match, to a farm or an aquarium. I believe that these experiences are all very important to be able to draw on for communication in later life. This would mean that the individual people would be far more able to compare things and draw from their experience (which would be very wide ranging under my curriculum), and be able to cope in any situation. A prime example is the situation we are in now, where we get science teachers who can't spell or write complex essays, and English teachers who need to use a calculator to count. Under my system, a brain surgeon would be able to raise sheep and a shepherd would be able to perform some basic ballet. However, a ballet dancer would not necessarily be able to do brain surgery, as it is too advanced to achieve without special training. They would have a good knowledge of first aid, though.

Robin, 17

〰〰〰

I think more time should be devoted to art, design and technology. I think we should go on more trips to local, national and international museums and art galleries. Well known artists should come into school on a regular basis. For example, a sculptor, a potter, a weaver, a metal worker, a painter and a graphic designer. Termly workshops should take place on pottery, mosaics, sculpting and so on.

Joseph, 9, Birmingham

〰〰〰

My destination is miles away from the tame, neatly cut habitats that many people never stray from. Clinging to their average lives with their average wives and husbands and their average houses with their average days out to the park with children and the dog. This gives them a sense of security, but it also closes the door to really learn. Open your eyes and you enter a world where you don't need to care about what other people think of you, all you need to do is learn … This world will not only make your brain grow, but it will cushion the harsh thoughts that an average person cannot help to think.

Anon.

〰〰〰

I have decided that our school should have four new subjects, including all the other subjects we have in school. These are my choices! N.W.O.L. (Natural Wildlife Outside Life). I think that our school should look at plants and wildlife and nature. This is because children should learn and research, figure out differences, identify colour, smell and shape. T.A.N.I.U. (Thread and Needle In Use). We don't get to learn how to do weaving because that's not what the teachers choose. SCULP-TURES. I have decided to choose this subject because I think that children have to learn how to model and what is modelling. FIRST AID. Start this subject. It is very important. If anyone gets injured, you could save their lives.

Fatema, primary, Surrey

〰〰〰

In my dream school, standards will be set for every child separately. I don't like the way children are expected to do this by seven and that by eleven, plus, if you have not achieved all those things by sixteen then you are told you won't get a decent job ever! This is very harmful to all children. The children who do well in exams think they're better than the kids who can't read! Surely we can't go on thinking like that!

Kate, secondary, London

〰〰〰

My dream school would be a school which would let me explore the world and tell me human knowledge. To achieve this ideal school would be located in three different places: underwater, underground and in space. At the start of every year, the children will choose the topics they are most interested in. (There are no compulsory time-tables.) Five professors will help the children in each place.

The underwater schools (in a giant submarine) will teach about marine life and communicating with fishes and marine mammals like dolphins. The sport lessons will be like treasure hunts: The professor will give a waterproof map of the underwater world to all the groups made by five children which will then go swimming under-water with a special equipment and try to find the treasure. The first group to succeed will get a prize! During the expedition, they will collect underwater plants and shells to make a collage in Art.

The underground school will consist of galleries and rooms dug at different depths inside the earth. It will allow you to study archaeology and geology. It will also allow you to learn how to do prehistoric paintings and as sport, practise speleology.

The space school will be a glass Dome built on Planet X which will allow you to see stars and constellations that are not visible from Earth. To reach the school you will travel in a special space shuttle that can go as fast as the speed of light. In the science class, using the latest technology, you will learn how to make a droid and then you will be allowed to make one yourself!!! In Art you will use electronic cir-cuits under a metal board to make a picture with flashing light.

The more I write about this school the more I want it to exist!!!

Gautier, primary, Oxford

〰〰〰

The school would keep animals like pigs so that children who wanted to be a farmer in the future could learn how to look after them.

Georgina, 8, Norfolk

〰〰〰

I think that Science should be introduced in primary School, and also practical subjects such as woodwork, cookery and perhaps general life skills, like how to iron a shirt and paint a cupboard! We could also do voluntary work with elderly people. I mean, if you were elderly, wouldn't you like someone to help you? General Knowledge periods could be introduced to expand pupil's knowledge of world politics and world affairs, history, music and art. After being to such a school, I am quite sure that we would all be as smart and knowledgeable as we possibly could be, and we may even be computer whizz kids as well.

Anon.

∽∾∽∾

The subject I like best is Science because I love doing experiments. I would like to know more about gases. I don't like French because I don't enjoy speaking it. What is the point why we must do French and German? It seems like a waste of time. In our area there is only 0.01% or less people from France and there is about 14% people like me who speak Urdu or Punjabi at home. In my ideal school there will be more science and people could choose which language they want to study.

Sofia, Lower Secondary, Huddersfield

∽∾∽∾

In my ideal school, the whole philosophy that dominates schools now will be dropped. It will be somewhere thriving with different personalities and gifts, where these things can be developed and used to help everyone else. We will no longer be treated as herds of an identical animal waiting to be civilised before we are let loose on the world. It will be recognised that it is our world too.

We will cease to be thought of as useless vessels waiting in disciplined conditions to be filled with our quota of information, just so we can regurgitate it all in exams so that our school looks good in the league tables. We will be thought of as individual people.

Miriam, 15, Reading

∽∾∽∾

The school I'd like would be one that was open, in all senses of the word.

First there would be plenty of air (trees, plants and gardens), but there would also be a spiritual openness and awareness which would come from each pupil being treated as unique.

In my school pupils would have freedom to choose lessons they wanted to do. One could if one wanted spend an entire week playing games, or doing art, or meeting top scientists and talking.

The school would also be much more integrated into the wider community. The notion of writing prize-winning essays on tropical rainforests without taking some action would be seen as strange. Schools would be part of the local and international community and would take part in solving some of its problems. This would re-attach effort to real tangible results and would have a positive effect on motivation to learn. It would mean pupils and teachers were not just working for some esoteric result.

Lastly my school would be holistic, education can often be divisive splitting subject from application and mind from soul. The education would be the best where art, music, maths and English blend and integrate and where one is not expected to forsake being a human being to teach or be taught.

Jonathan, 17, Manchester

∽∾∽∾

My ideal school would be an entire planet. The planet would be divided into four sections. Each section would have several main aspects similar to each of them. Each section would be composed of a specific terrain, with its own different culture and way of life for the inhabitants, and a wide variety of wildlife species individual to that particular zone. In each section would be a large telescope to view the terrain. It would also be used to view planet Earth and to send light signals as messages to the pupils' homes.

The four sections would be Desert; Underwater; Mountains and Volcanoes; and Jungle. Students would travel in large groups of mixed ages to promote social inter-action and respect, and lessen the age divides. The pupils would spend a year in each section and once they had gained sufficient knowledge of the area they would be tested and move onto the next section and a different group.

In each section the pupils would learn a variety of skills, but the focal point of the zones would be life experiences. They would experience different climates and terrain, learn to identify with different cultures and encounter many character-building experiences. They would experience first hand all that they need in life rather than being confined to classrooms. Pupils would learn life and survival skills particular to each zone, for example in the mountain zone pupils would learn altitude sickness precautions. In this way pupils would learn basic theories for survival, and how to use natural features to the best of their advantage.

Some subjects would also be integrated into life skills. Geography would be the knowledge and exploration of the terrain and natural features. Each zone would have its own assigned language so the pupils would leave school with a variety of lan-guages, which had all been encountered as a way of life. Social economics would be combined into cultural integration and overcoming differences. Pupils would also learn how to handle wildlife.

After the year spent in a zone each pupil would have to undergo two tests – of courage and physical skills, ingenuity in a situation; and of mental skills – intellectual knowledge of the terrain and how to survive on natural resources. The latter would be sat as a paper; the former would be an active exam taken in the zone. These tests would be done as an individual to test personal resourcefulness. Another test would be taken in groups to test for co-operation; and leadership and teamwork skills.

In this way all students gain:

    Knowledge of each terrain
    Experience in the real world
    Self realisation and character building
    Teamwork skills – Self motivation and appreciation
    Life skills – How to adapt knowledge to use in situations and put into practice

Pupils would have a holiday to spend on earth with their family at the completion of each zone.

When all four zones are completed the pupils are in sixth form. They move to a base in the centre of the planet. Here they would learn to appreciate their homeland, planet Earth, and how to care for it – environmental issues. They would also further their education in such areas as philosophy, history, theology and literature – the human culture.

This means that everyone turned out from school is tested to be worthy to live on planet Earth, and capable of survival without such methods as cars and other polluting feats of engineering. They would research environmentally friendly methods of travel and other necessities. All inhabitants of Earth will have successfully learnt how to live in harmony with nature. In the sixth form it is possible to return to any zone, to live or coach new pupils as a specialist. There are rewards for completing the four zones, in the centre of the planet there would be luxuries such as virtual reality resources and antigravity rooms. The planet would be called Scholastica (see Plate 7).

Cara, 14, Winchester

∽∽∽

In the present state system, there is a set curriculum that is concerned with efficiency, rather than fulfilment. It prioritises the preparation of a useful workforce, and makes little allowance for individual preference and talent. Although it could be argued that children need a balanced education in order to keep their options open, I think that timetables are too inflexible. It may well be beneficial for some students to specialise earlier in accordance with their own interests. The main reason for this is that I feel that all people should have freedom as to what they learn. I think that the mind is one thing over which the individual should have full rights, and should not be subject to invasion by others' ideas of what they should know.

There is a tendency for some important subjects not to be offered in many schools. Such subjects as Psychology, Sociology, Politics and Philosophy are rarely offered at GCSE, but I personally think that they are the most important, thought provoking subjects of all (I have studied Sociology at A level). This may be a subjective judgement, but these subjects all have something in common that may be responsible for their neglect. They may all be perceived as 'dangerous', as they can incite people to think freely and originally, and possibly to challenge the school's authority. A good system need not fear analysis and scrutiny.

There are guidelines as to the way in which the information is to be presented. Usually, teaching is supposed to be objective, but there are some areas where this is clearly not so. For instance, in Citizenship lessons, teachers must 'promote heterosexual marriage'. This could be damaging to pupils of some backgrounds and orientations, and may have bad effects on social tolerance.

The school I'd like would:

- Have no rigid curriculum, only guidelines for students and teachers
- Endeavour to be as objective as possible, allowing pupils to form their own views
- Replace school assemblies with debates – open (and optional) to all
- Be tolerant toward different types of language use, trying not to penalise class or ethnic variations
- Offer subjects such as Psychology, Sociology, Politics and Philosophy
- Allow students to choose their own subjects.

Lorna, 14, Ipswich

Chapter 5

Learning

'Let us out ... !'

Schools are key forces in the reproduction of inequalities in society as they perform their function of sifting and selecting, awarding and failing. Learning becomes limited to a pre-selected and served up curriculum (Apple, 1995). Children and young people in school today are more likely than ever to recognise these processes that touch their lives everyday. More than the school pupils who contributed their ideas on learning to the first competition, they are subject to a regulated and statutory curriculum which limits the possibilities for flexibility in classroom practice. The 1988 Education Reform Act in England and Wales, in generating an educational market place and imposing a curriculum, has strengthened the subordinate position of pupils in schools (Wyness, 2000). In spite of the rhetoric of inclusion, which argues that children and young people share a right to a common educational environment in which all are valued equally, the principles of marketisation work against such being achieved (Armstrong, 1999: 76). The commentary offered by children and young people in the 'School I'd Like', 2001 collection, reflects a concern that learning is becoming increasingly limited in schools today by administrative and social structures.

Metaphors of schooling are revealing for what they tell us about how school functions as part of a larger ideological project. 'Drill' was a term used extensively in schools at the beginning of the twentieth century, an activity associated with the maintenance of military discipline. 'Drill' was gradually replaced by the term 'exercise', implying repetition, practice and activity which the learner might view as tedious but carries out anyway either under duress or in the belief that personal benefit will be achieved in the long term. The 'exercise book' was a familiar technology to those educated in post-war Britain. Today, the term 'exercise' has been replaced by the term 'work' in describing and assigning to children tasks to carry out in classrooms and beyond. Children take 'work' home; the 'worksheet' is ubiquitous at all levels and across all subjects of the curriculum; pupils are expected to develop 'work' habits. 'Get on with your work' is a phrase most often used by teachers in addressing pupils. Classrooms are 'managed' and teachers are assessed for their management skills and are rewarded for their 'productivity'. The metaphor of the factory which accompanied the development of state education from its beginnings at the end of the nineteenth century has gradually been replaced by the metaphor of the corporation, company or firm. Parents 'invest' in their children's future, looking for a good return on their outlay. The language of the corporation or business is all about results, on turning out a product, on quantifying improvement. Learning has become a commodity, 'a thing rather than an activity ... that can be amassed and measured, the possession of which is a measure of the productivity of the individual within the society' (Illich, cited in Gajardo, 1994: 715). Alfie Kohn, writing about schooling in the USA, has reminded us that 'The process of learning is more import-ant than the products that result. To use the language of "work" or, worse, to adopt a business-style approach to school reform, is to reverse those priorities' (Kohn, 1997: 1). The language and metaphors of schooling, together with an uncritical intro-duction of computer technology into classrooms, and the emphasis on consumerism, work against the possibilities of the school functioning as a site promoting global sustainability and eco-justice (Bowers, 2000).

But in fact, learning, like play, is a natural activity in childhood. There are biolo-gical and neurological impulses towards learning that children are not entirely con-scious of but occur as part of growth and development. Early educators such as Pestalozzi, Montessori and Dewey believed strongly that one of the most important roles of a teacher is to create or adapt an environment which does not fetter this natural process and to know when to stand back and allow such natural activity to take place (Pestalozzi, 1894; Montessori, 1912). However, the routines of traditional schooling, and particularly the language of reward and punishment, indicate a belief that the child will only learn under certain imposed conditions and rather like an adult will only work under duress. Children recognise this paradox and in their alternative visions remind the adult world of their natural proclivity to learn.

One commentary, describing an imagined school of the future, challenges the current assumption that children must be forced to learn.

> In this school, lessons are not strictly divided by subjects. Most of the time, lessons in Math, English, Geography or Science can be taught as one. Students learn concepts by doing – seeing, smelling, hearing, touching, and tasting as well as thinking either cre-atively or logically. All their senses are utilized in all sorts of manners so that learning is meaningful and practical – not something so alien that they have to be forced upon to do. When children find learning meaningful, they will naturally want to learn more and hence, they will be self-motivated and do not need to be pushed by adults to learn.
>
> Oliver, 13, Loughborough

The school, as traditionally conceived, is only one possible site of learning. There has been a massive growth in the cultural and leisure industries in recent years which has spawned a new generation of 'interactive' learning environments visited by children with other family members outside of school time. Gardens, museums, nature reserves, galleries and ecological centres often employ education officers whose job it is to liaise with schools and to enhance the educational impact of the site. These developments have led some to consider what the experience of children and their families when visiting such sites can tell us about alternative contexts of learning.

The Eden Project in Cornwall, opened in 2001, is a garden theme park consisting of several bio domes containing representations of the world's eco zones. When school groups visit such sites, they can be observed to adapt classroom-style, task-oriented approaches which contrast with the 'natural learning behaviours' manifested by family groups visiting at weekends (Griffin and Symington, 1997). Such behaviours tend to be less formally organised, more random and led by curiosity rather than design. It has been argued that school-imposed task structures inhibit the natural tendency to learn at such sites. 'Worksheets encouraged "tunnel vision", box-ticking and emphasis on literacy rather than environmental objectives' and surveys have indicated that 'most teachers and pupils felt that learning would have been more effective if there had been unstructured time for exploration, open-ended questioning and consolidation through structured discussion' (Peacock, 2002: 10).

The comments of children about their ideal learning environment unite across time with the cry 'Let us out!'. For some this means having more opportunity to learn outside of school boundaries, to see, touch, smell and feel real artefacts or nature (Plate 7). Many children dream of escaping the confines of the walled and windowed classroom to learn in the school grounds or in special open-air classrooms designed for the purpose. Blishen found that children were:

> begging that they be allowed to *get out* of the dead air of the classroom – to be freed from that sterile and cramped learning situation in which the teacher, the text book and the examination-dominated syllabus have decided what should be learnt, and how it should be learnt, and that virtually everything should be presented as a hurried intellectual abstraction.
>
> (1969: 55)

Once more, the tediousness of lessons, the failure of teachers to inspire and the boring methods to communicate facts are criticised. However, no one reading the thousands of entries gathered in the archive can be left with any doubt that children want to learn and they believe that changes in the organisation, design and structure of education can allow learning to happen more readily.

Often, the detailed suggestions offered for change are almost identical to those offered in the 1969 collection. The metaphor of the university or 'city of learning' was used to explain how learning could be supported, as in this 1969 example.

> My ideal school would be run on the lines of the present university system. There would be no classrooms but lecture theatres; after each lecture the students would have to attend a discussion group consisting of a teacher and five students. In this discussion group they would discuss the ideas put over in the lecture.
>
> Boy, 16

An idea of the school as a 'city of learning' is captured in many of the images which form a large part of the 2001 'School I'd Like' archive (see, for example, Plate 1). Such imagery challenges the dominant metaphors of schooling and with it the organisation of learning which is driven by market forces.

There is much anxiety expressed today about the state of childhood and of public schooling. Much of the blame for the 'crises' in education, both in the UK and USA, is placed on the individual child or its immediate family. Children are perceived to be a threat in our schools and the media relishes every opportunity to report on disruption or violence perpetrated by ever-younger children. The way that learning is organised and understood to take place in schools is not usually recognised to be at the heart of the problem but, on the contrary, the solution. 'Children at Risk' is a term we do not associate with places of learning or with schools. Rather, as anthropologist Sharon Stevens suggests, schools increasingly regard children as 'the risk' to the survival of school as a historical project (Stevens, in Giroux, 2000: 9). But the responses of children here, which focus on how learning is experienced in schools today, do suggest that children are indeed at risk. The risk is that their experience of school will permanently dampen their natural proclivity for learning, and the enjoyment and fulfilment that learning brings.

Children and young people in the 2001 'Schools I'd Like' competition present a challenge to the individualist thrust of current educational policy. These individual voices suggest a strong solidarity and collective consciousness, a sense of belonging to a collective culture. Very few entries contain individual gripes or moans but, rather, speak with empathy about the way that school fails their fellow learners. Time and again, children express how changes might take place to help their fellows succeed and to improve learning for all children. Testing, measuring and examining individuals and encouraging competition is, as it was in the past, criticised strongly and seen for what it is: a means by which the state benefits and, through which, schooling becomes divorced from learning.

In the 1969 publication, *The School That I'd Like*, Blishen commented on the way that young people had viewed learning. He recognised:

> Great hatred of subject barriers simply as devices that break up the school day into a series of small dissociated experiences! Detestation of bells that ring just as you have may have become interested in what you are doing ... [which] makes the day such a frustrating patchwork.
>
> (1969: 83)

He recognised alongside the children who participated in the competition that,

> when things are chopped up like this ... you can't anywhere put down real roots. And the children want to put down roots, deep into human learning.
>
> (1969: 83)

Much has changed since the late 1960s in the way learning is organised in schools, but not in the direction that young people had advocated, which was to fundamentally question subject barriers, create new kinds of integrated topic-based curricula and bring about a 'new flexibility of routine out of which might come learning as a coherent experience' (ibid.: 84).

Children today have offered suggestions for practical changes that might improve and enhance the experience and enjoyment of learning. There is recognition that expertise and wisdom reside not only in those individuals trained as teachers, but also in the wider community. One can see parallels with the pedagogy advocated by John Dewey (1916) and the de-schooling learning webs advocated by Ivan Illich (1973). More specialists and those whose working lives depend on their knowledge should be invited to instruct children in schools. Parents, grandparents and others in the community should be welcomed into schools to teach, learn or observe learning taking place.

Learning will happen with ease when it is allowed to be fun and when children are regarded less as 'herds of identical animals', but as individuals who are made comfortable in mind, body and spirit. Part of the sense of comfort and stimulation will result from being granted some control, choice and direction in their learning. Children and young people long to be allowed more activity, experimentation and continuity in the task; once started, they want to be allowed to finish. A recent study comparing secondary school pupil experience of learning in three European countries, Denmark, France and England, found that the English children 'enjoyed school and lessons the least and were the most likely to want to leave school as soon as they could and to feel that school got in the way of their lives' (Osborn, 2002: 274). The same study found that an important cross cultural 'constant' among young people was the pupils' concern that learning should be active and that lessons should have an element of 'fun' or humour.

The young people who took part in the original competition would have been horrified had they been able to see 34 years into the future, that children in schools would be voicing the exact same concerns as theirs. The continuity is remarkable, even as far as detailed commentary. Take, for example, this:

> The English lesson could be so interesting if only it were allowed to be. Instead of a book of *Macbeth*, why don't we go to see *Macbeth*, and then discuss it afterwards, but let us recognise and understand the plot before we start.
>
> Lynne, 15

And compare with this from the 2001 study:

> I adore Shakespeare, well I adore Shakespeare tragedies, but I wouldn't dream of reading one through slowly in this day and age, not as an approach to it. I reach for a decent video with a straight down the middle performance, read the synopsis on the box, and I watch the video with the text alongside me, straight through, beginning to end. Then I watch other versions of the same play and imagine myself into my own production ... And yet I know schools who advise their pupils not to watch a video until they've studied the play by which time many pupils are so bogged down in all sorts of things that they've been told, so lost in a forest of trees that they can't take a fresh look at it.
>
> Hero Joy, 14

Perhaps in 1967 the youngsters held out more hope for change than their counterparts today who appear to understand much about the barriers to change. But children now recognise that school is not by any means the only place of learning and voice recognition that, with the application of electronic devices such as televisions and computers, home-based learning offers advantages over the restricted regime of the school. Once again, enough time to learn and to see a task through to its completion is an attraction, suggesting that children are often frustrated in the timetabling demands placed upon them.

Further reading

Apple, M.W. (1995) *Education and Power*, 2nd edn, London: Routledge.

Armstrong, F. (1999) 'Inclusion, curriculum and the struggle for space in school', *International Journal of Inclusive Education*, 3, 1, 75–87.

Blishen, E. (1969) *The School That I'd Like*, London: Penguin.

Bowers, C.A. (2000) 'Toward eco-justice pedagogy'. Paper presented at the European Educational Research Association Conference, Edinburgh, 20–23 September.

Brunner, J. (1996) *The Culture of Education*, Cambridge, MA: Harvard University Press.

Dewey, J. (1916) *Democracy and Education. An Introduction to the Philosophy of Education* (1966 edn.), New York, NY: Free Press.

Gajardo, M. (1994) 'Ivan Illich', in Morsy, Z. (ed.) *Key Thinkers in Education, Volume 2*, Paris: UNESCO Publishing.

Giroux, H.A. (2000) *Stealing Innocence*, New York, NY: Palgrave.

Griffin, J. and Symington, D. (1997) 'Moving from task-oriented to learning-oriented strategies on school excursions to museums', *Science Education*, 81, 763–79.

Illich, I. (1973) *Deschooling Society*, Harmondsworth: Penguin.

Kohn, A. (1997) 'Students don't "work" – they learn', *Education Week*, 3 September. Online: available at: http://www.alfiekohn.org/teaching/edweek/sdwtl.htm (accessed October 2002).

Montessori, M. (1912) *The Montessori method*, New York, NY: F.A. Stokes Company Inc.

Osborn, M. (2001) 'Constants and contexts in pupil experience of learning and schooling: comparing learners in England, France and Denmark', *Comparative Education*, 37, 3, 267–78.

Peacock, A. (2002) 'Making the environmental message more effective: working with children for ecological awareness at the Eden Project'. Paper presented at the 'Beyond Anthropocentrism' Conference at the University of Exeter, 16–17 July.

Pestalozzi, J.H. (1894) *How Gertrude Teaches her Children*, translated by Lucy, E. Holland and Frances C. Turner, London: Swan Sonnenschein.

Wyness, M.G. (2000) 'Sex education and the teaching of citizenship: towards a more inclusive conception of childhood', *Pedagogy, Culture and Society*, 8, 3, 245–63.

Learning

In the pretty, lively school there are lots of different classes. There are language lessons on French and German, also there are maths and history lessons. You can go to whatever class you feel like any day. The teachers are kind and interested in the children's ideas . . . The most important thing is learning is fun.

Alix, 7, Oxford

I think we could learn a lot more if we had smaller class sizes of about 20. If you had smaller class sizes then you could have more one on one. You could also have specialist teachers in to teach us, for example in cookery if we were making cakes then we could get a person in to teach us who actually makes cakes for a living.

Helen, 12, Gosforth

Some parents or grandparents didn't have the facilities or technology when they were at school which is why I think that once a week they should be able to come into school and learn about some of the new teaching methods in the curriculum with their children.

Christie, 12, Gosforth

Learning can be thirsty work and to keep the minds of pupils working, they would be offered refreshments to relax the student at work feeding the imagination as well as listening to music to soothe and stimulate the brain.

Stacey, 13, Stoke Golding

My ideal school would be a fun environment to learn in. For example in some schools, the walls, corridors and halls are often quite drab making the pupil miserable thus affecting their grades. If there were to be bright colours on the walls, carpets, ceilings etc pupils would feel happier and more in control of what they were doing enabling their grades to rise. It probably encourage pupils to learn more, much faster. Pupils would also feel happier to come to school. Lessons could be taught using games methods for fun. This would also help the things needed to be learnt stick in the pupils' mind for longer as they would have something to remember it by!

Nadia, 12, Chertsey

For learning instead of a blackboard there will be a 1 m 16 cm by 2 m 39 cm television. The T.V. will be turned into sky digital and all David Attenborough video collections so we can learn about wildlife. Each pupil will have a laptop with built in security system.

Joe, 9, Clacton-on-Sea

I want more homework.

Hannah, 4, Barnsley

An academic city of learning

This new school will be almost like a university as we will have the freedom of choice and opinion, not treated as mobs of classes, but as individuals. Naturally more teachers will be needed to cater for such a large school, they however will be trained accordingly and learn to treat us as individuals. We will have a couple of largish assignments per week, not every night. These will be set in lectures that we will go to also on choice yet we must go to a certain number of these per week. You may not choose to stay at the school–college but many will, as there will be a home like atmosphere around the place with rooms sharing almost like proper apartments. We will of course go home at weekends. At the college there will be plenty for us to do as the facilities will be infinite. The campus will have many, many things to make it welcoming and yet exciting at the same time. There will be shops where we may purchase items on already purchased cards (a lot like a credit card). To go with the shops, food diners, gyms, sport facilities, cinemas and even places to skate. This will also add to the great atmosphere at this academic city of learning. The place will be flooded with happy pupils walking, talking and generally enjoying themselves at this multimedia learning haven. There will be a whole new kind of system as far as tests, exams and other work is concerned. You see the main source of stress nowadays in teenagers is work and revision. That's why thanks to 'super skool' all this is forgotten. There will be a new system in town. Say goodbye to GCSE's and A-level's. Because in the school of the future we will be marked all through the year and be given a final grade at the end. This new system is perfect as it will reduce stress, due to exams, and will also reduce poor behaviour as the pupil will know that he is being constantly marked on diligence as well as achievement.

Alexi, 14, Coventry

∽∽∽

The School I'd like ... could slow down a little occasionally. They all speak too fast. Some of the children can sign and all of the staff do but it's all usually too fast. Normal schooling is very heavily based on hearing and reading the English language. There are too many words and too many letters. I can understand key words and simple sentences. It is really helpful if I can see a photograph, an object of reference, a symbol and signs accompanied by hearing the sound of the word. The school I'd like could do more sensory things, more hands on, more touchy/feely. Everyone has loads of senses. We can feel with different parts of our body, we can see, hear, taste, smell. How many senses does the national curriculum focus on? Sometimes I find life in the classroom boring and sometimes the pace is too fast and I switch off. Well, who wouldn't – day in, day out, literacy hour, numeracy hour, registration. How about smelling hour, tactile hour, music hour and physical activity hour. What about employing Charlie Dimmock to fill the school with wonderful water features that we could see, hear, touch, smell and feel?

Hugh, 6 (with help from his mum), Wellington

∽∽∽

There would be more of creative arts, so that students can take the opportunity to express themselves.

Megan, 13, Warminster

∽∽∽

One change that we would make would be to in summer have some lessons outside. In summer in a classroom you get hot and bored. Outside we would be a lot happier and work harder. There could be special outside areas in the school grounds with tables and chairs and the teacher could book lessons there.

Alex, Jessica and Sarah, 12 and 13, Oakhampton

∽∽∾

School is a very important part in a child's life. Not only does it help them learn but it helps them to grow up, learn how to work together and also to socialise. If I could change things about our school things would be very different indeed . . .

It is always good to learn a bit extra out of classes so my ideal school would be if we had a study room during break to do homework. Of course, if you enjoy your break, and wouldn't want to miss it then you could go after school to be picked up later. There would also be an I.T. room to help when you go to secondary school or even when you start work. With all this learning business you want to know that my school has its sporty side. A two storey high building with the bottom swimming and the top netball and football you can't go wrong. Art can take all different levels but each class will get to draw the surroundings of the school. With the new trees that would be planted around a big patch of grass in the middle, would be a room called the glass room. The glass room has glass as its walls so you can see every tree. This is because of the horrible English weather so when it rains you can still draw the trees.

Parents always want to know what is happening at school. Apart from evenings where parents look at children's work they don't have a clue on what is going on. So every Thursday parents can come in and sit at the back of the classroom and watch the goings-on in the classroom. This enables them to help children with their home-work by knowing what they had been taught and to find out how their child behaves at school.

Lauren, lower secondary, Romford

∽∽∾

Trips, Let's go!
We all love trips, and we can learn so much from going and seeing things. Numeracy hour and literacy hour can be boring. LET US OUT!

The teachers and the children would love more organised outings, but I bet the department of Education says no. In other countries the less formal approach is very successful, so why not give it a go?

Kimberley, 11, Swanwick

∽∽∾

I know you have to come to school to learn but what's the point when you can learn on television . . . My ideal school would be not coming.

Robert, 12, Crewe

∽∽∾

All day for work, we would write publishing stories, and send them to book-shops. At the moment we only write stories on very few occasions, and they never get published.

Clare, 11, Cardiff

∽∽∾

The place must be unafraid of kids staring out of windows and must not insist on 100% attention or even 100% attendance … It is a terrible pressure for kids to have to pay attention and think what they are told to think. I would encourage people to dream more and enjoy the sun and the sky, the growing grass and the bear boughed trees. I would encourage kids to look beyond the classroom, out of the classroom and see themselves doing different things.

Hero Joy, home educated, 14, Kent

〰〰〰

The best thing about the maths classroom is that when our teacher enters, hundreds of sparkling numbers tumble down from the ceiling and then disappear as they hit the floor. And all of us scurry around clutching nets in our hands, trying to catch them. If you're quick enough, you might find you've caught the golden number which gives you the answer to that day's homework.

Jade, 9, London

〰〰〰

Pupils will decide what they want to learn and learn it. Each pupil will work on their own projects, producing them in any way they like. They will then have something to be proud of. They will receive help from people working at the school and fellow pupils, as everyone will be seen as having valid knowledge and opinions. Books and resources will be available and pupils can go to relevant places, or meet with experts. They will not be 'taken' anywhere – they will arrange trips etc. themselves. Each project, when it is finished, will be handed in; not to be marked (after all how can someone be entitled to invade work with red ink and brand it with a letter of the alphabet?) but to teach others about what the pupil has learned.

Because everyone will be learning different things there will be no set classes. Pupils will not be expected to work with and like others just because they were all born between the same two dates. Students will be able to choose where and with whom they work.

I must admit to my share of graffiti on the science lab gas taps as sixty students have gathered (and have spent half an hour being herded) around a desk to watch water boil. If the teacher had simply recognised that we were people with brains she would have realised that we all knew what water looks like while boiling. She could have said 'When water boils …' and got on with the lesson, instead of driving me to the frustration it takes to write 'Get me out of this f***ing dump' in pencil, not even caring about the possibility of her wrath if caught. (Fortunately my comment went unnoticed amongst all the other clumsily worded cries for salvation that decorated the physics lab.)

Miriam, 15, Reading

〰〰〰

When we were doing the Vikings in history, we didn't see any of their weapons up close we only saw them in pictures. It would be better if we were taken to a museum to see them. We should be taken on trips as part of our topics, it would help us understand more.

Richard, 12, Glasgow

〰〰〰

This place of learning should never be somewhere to fear, nor should it restrict free speech and ideas, or be somewhere which will strip you of the confidence and individuality you need to succeed in life. School is there to prepare you for your future life, not to make you scared of it. My ideal school is a community, which upholds your strong points and overcomes your weak points. Teachers should always know how much they should be involved in your private life, but they refrain from depriving you of a life outside school untainted by the shackles of school work.

What is education if it is not about people? If results are what the government wants, then replace every child with a robot each one the same, producing the same work, the same results year after year. Education should be working to make people valuable citizens, not so called 'valuable statistics'.

Angela, 15, Croydon

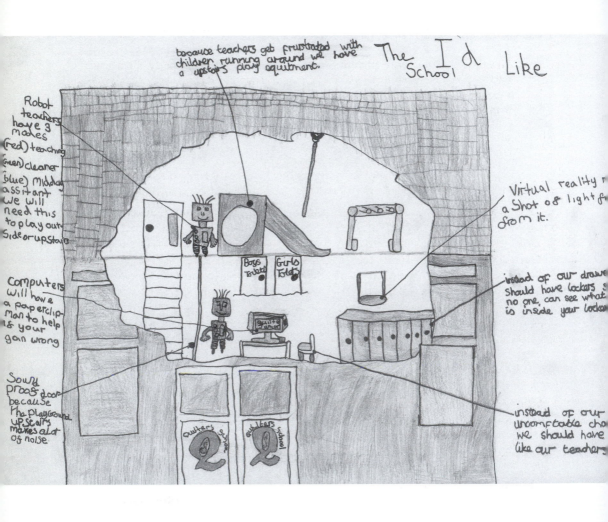

The School I'd Like

because teachers get frustrated with children running around we have a upstairs play equipment.

Robot teachers have 3 modes (red) teaching (green) cleaner (blue) Middae assistant we will need this to play outside or upstairs

Virtual reality a shot of light from it.

Computers will have a paperclip man to help is your gan wrong

instead of our drawers should have lockers so no one can see what is inside your locker

Sound proof door because the playground upstairs makes a lot of noise.

Boys Toilets   Girls Toilets

quilters school   quilters school

instead of our uncomfortable chair we should have like our teachers

Chapter 6

Teachers and special people

'Nobody forgets a good teacher ...'

> All words have the 'taste' of a profession, a genre, a tendency, a party, a particular work, a particular person, a generation, an age group, the day and hour. Each word tastes of the context in which it has lived its socially charged life: all words and forms are populated by intentions.
>
> (Bakhtin, 1986: 293)

It is 1999 and a 30-second government sponsored teacher recruitment film is playing in English cinemas. A young boy in a school uniform lies, arms outstretched on the sand. There are books around him, their pages blowing in the wind. Cut to a classroom. There are rows of neatly dressed, well-behaved children, black and white, looking in rapt attention at their teacher, eyes misty and mouths open. The teacher smiles as he winds up a model of the Wright brothers' flying machine. The children imagine a monochrome scene of joy as the Kitty Hawk took to the sky. Mood music swells as the children twirl little wooden propellers into the air, demonstrating the theory of flight. The message: 'nobody forgets a good teacher.' The question: a good teacher sets the imagination free – could you inspire young minds? Move forward four years to a *Guardian* newspaper report on the 'Teaching Awards 2002':

> A newly qualified English teacher described as 'weird, wacky and wonderful' by her students ... was named last night as one of 10 top teachers in England, Wales and Northern Ireland in the national teaching awards.
>
> She said she had entered teaching with a strong sense of herself and what she wanted to do: 'It just sounds clichéd but you can make a difference, and I wanted to do that, and I love my subject ... I just realised how powerful somebody can be if they are a good communicator. I want everybody to have that opportunity to be powerful.
>
> (Smithers, 2002)

Teachers represent a powerful force in society. They are invested with authority to guide the learner's journey towards knowledge and habits of thinking which determine future identities. Not surprisingly, given this position, images of teachers are pervasive in popular culture. In particular, there are a number of enduring cultural images of teachers at work – the caring female teacher in the classroom, the inspiring 'hero' teacher (Joseph and Burnaford, 1994; Bicklen, 1995; Weber and Mitchell,

1995; Keroes, 1999). The circulation of such images – through films, television, novels – is so extensive that 'even before children begin school, they have already been exposed to a myriad of images of teachers ... which have made strong and lasting impressions on them' (Weber and Mitchell, 1995: 2). There is also a huge amount of research literature on 'teachers', with many disciplines and sub-disciplines claiming 'teachers' as their own (Acker, 1995/96, 1999). Central to much of this research is a concern with the relational dimension of teaching – teachers with teachers, teachers with managers, teachers with parents and, of course, teachers with pupils.

It came as no surprise, therefore, to find descriptions of teachers dominating many of the entries in the 2001 competition. Children wrote at length about their experiences of teachers, and their yearning for certain qualities to be present in all future teachers.

Blishen found a similar level of yearning in 'hundreds' of essays, a yearning based on a grievance 'made so insistently, and by so many' that teachers were remote authoritative individuals. He subsequently drew up a list of the qualities which children wished their teachers had:

> [They should] be understanding ... and patient; should encourage and praise wherever possible; should listen to their pupils, and give their pupils a chance to speak; should be willing to have points made against them, be humble, kind, capable of informality, simply pleasant; should share more activities with their children than they commonly do, and should not expect all children to be always docile. They should have a conscience about the captive nature of their audience; should attempt to establish links with parents; should be punctual for lessons; enthusiastic within reason; should not desert a school lightly; should recognise the importance to a child of being allowed to take the initiative in school work; and above all, should be warm and personal.
>
> (Blishen, 1969: 129–31)

All of these listed teacher qualities can be found in the 2001 data, but are also evidenced in 1990s educational research about teacher–pupil relations in the UK (Clark and Trafford, 1995; Lightbody et al., 1996; Bleach, 1997) and appear to be consistent across a range of variables: school provision – at primary and secondary levels, and in special education (Garner 1993; Pollard, 1996; Younger and Warrington, 1999) – and gender and ethnicity (Milosevic, 1996; Schaechter, Grosvenor and Faust, 2000).

Blishen located many of the criticisms levelled at teachers by children with the failure of the education system, and observed that 'to be the teacher the children desired' required 'enormous changes in the whole system'. In short, for Blishen (and the children in his study) there was a need for 'a new kind of teaching and a new kind of teacher' (Blishen, 1969: 131). In the last 25 years or more, there has been an enormous increase in statutory legislation in England and Wales relating to education. Indeed, Judd asked during a debate on the Education Act 1994 'whether there is now a constitutional requirement that there should be an annual Education Bill' (quoted in Hinds, 1995: 79). The education and training of teachers, in particular, has been the focus of successive government's policy initiatives. Statutory regulations governing Initial Teacher Training (ITT) have undergone seven major revisions since 1984 (Welch and Mahoney, 2000: 141; Grosvenor and Myers, 2001: 284). Entrance to the profession is determined by the success of student teachers in achieving a mandatory set of competence statements or QTS (Qualified Teacher Status) standards (DfEE Circular, 4/98). The standards focus on achieving the subject knowledge and craft skills necessary to teach and assess the National Curriculum and are written in generic not subject–specific terms. They provide a baseline for further professional standards relating to induction and performance threshold. The QTS standards were developed with the professed aim of ensuring that:

> All new teachers know how to equip pupils with the experience and understanding they need to play their part in a socially just society, including through appropriate moral, cultural, social and spiritual development.
>
> (Teacher Training Agency, 2000: 9)

It has been argued that in school reform the time lapse between policy conception and changes in schooling is 'long' (Cuban, 1995). A 'new kind of teacher' may be slowly appearing in the system, but the degree of criticism expressed by young people in 2001 cannot be ignored. Moreover, the driving force behind the reforms in teacher education is public accountability. Student teachers are trained to enter a community of practice where the authority of standards is used to evaluate performance and where performance in turn is viewed as a key mechanism for improving pupil achievement (Ball, 2001; Fielding, 2001). Husbands has deconstructed the performance model now in place in schools in England and Wales:

> School targets can be derived from national targets; and teacher and pupil targets from school targets. In the short term, it is almost certain that the sharper focus and defined targets brought by performance management systems will deliver higher levels of attainment in external tests and examinations ... It is less clear that the structures of performance management will in the medium term produce a 'nation equipped for the challenges and opportunities of the new millennium'.
>
> (2001: 11)

The inputs, processes and outputs of this performance model are narrowly conceived and are unlikely to 'equip pupils with the experience and understanding they need to play their part in a socially just society' (Teacher Training Agency, 2000: 9). Finally, there may be attempts to bring children into the process of performance accountability – OFSTED piloted the use of pupil questionnaires in primary and secondary schools as an evaluative tool for teacher performance in the autumn of 2002 (Woodward, 2002) – but, as stated earlier in this book, children have no illusions about their voices being heard in school, let alone acted upon.

Everyone *does* remember a good teacher, but it sadly appears to be the case that negative experiences of teacher–pupil relations are still widespread in UK schools. That said, it is ironic that while children are teachers' most severe critics they are also their greatest advocates. Like Blishen's children, those of 2001 saw teachers as important and the majority could not see them replaced by machines. The children of 2001 recognised the heavy demands being made on teachers today and the effects of those demands on their personalities and health; and they offer practical statements of support – better pay, improved staff room facilities, stress management, shorter hours, increased teacher supply. In sum, at the beginning of a new millennium, one can say that children care about their teachers.

Further reading

Acker, S. (1995/96) 'Gender and teachers' work', *Review of Research in Education*, 21, 99–162.

Acker, S. (1999) *The Realities of Teacher Work. Never a Dull Moment*, London: Cassell.

Bakhtin, M.M. (1986) *The Dialogic Imagination*, translated by C. Emerson and M. Holquist, Austin, TX: University of Texas Press.

Ball, S. (2001) 'Performativities and fabrications in the education economy: towards the performative society', in Gleeson, D. and Husbands, C. (eds) *The Performing School: Managing, Teaching and Learning in a Performance Culture*, London: Falmer Press.

Biklen, S.K. (1995) *School Work*, Albany, NY: State University of New York Press.

Bleach, K. (1997) 'Where did we go wrong?' *Times Educational Supplement*, 4207, 14 February, 14.

Blishen, E. (1969) *The School That I'd Like*, London: Penguin.

Clark, A. and Trafford, J. (1995) 'Boys into modern languages: an investigation of the discrepancy in attitudes and performance between boys and girls in modern languages', *Gender and Education*, 7, 3, 315–25.

Cuban, L. (1995) 'The myth of failed school reform', *Education Week*, 1 November. Online: available at: http://www.edweek.org/ew/ewstory.html (accessed 18 October 2002).

DfEE (1998) (Circular 4/98) *Teaching: High Status, High Standards, Annex A*, London: DfEE.

Fielding, M. (2001) 'Target setting, policy pathology and student perspectives: learning to labour in new times', in Fielding, M. (ed.) *Taking Labour Really Seriously: Four Years Hard Labour*, London: Falmer.

Garner, P. (1993) 'What disruptive pupils say about the school curriculum and the way it is taught', *Therapeutic Care and Education*, 2, 3, 404–15.

Grosvenor, I. and Myers, K. (2001) 'Engaging with history after Macpherson', *The Curriculum Journal*, 12, 3, 275–89.

Hinds, W. (1995) 'The Education Act 1994 – the teacher training provisions', *Education and the Law*, 7, 2, 79–90.

Husbands, C. (2001) 'Managing "performance" in the performing school', in Gleeson, D. and Husbands, C. (eds) *The Performing School: Managing, Teaching and Learning in a Performance Culture*, London: Falmer Press.

Joseph, P.B. and Burnaford, G.E. (eds) (1994) *Images of Schoolteachers in Twentieth-Century America – Paragons, Polarities, Complexities*, New York, NY: St. Martin's Press.

Keroes, J. (1999) *Tales Out of School. Gender, Longing and the Teacher in Fiction and Film*, Carbondale, IL: Southern Illinois University Press.

Lightbody, P., Siann, G., Stocks, R. and Walsh, D., *et al.* (1996) 'Motivation and attribution at secondary school: an empirical study', *British Educational Research Journal*, 18, 3, 221–34.

Milosevic, L. (1996) 'Pupils' experience of P.E. questionnaire results', *British Journal of Physical Education*, 27, 1, 16–20.

Pollard, A. (1996) 'Playing the system? Pupil perspectives on curriculum and pedagogy and assessment in primary schools', in Croll, P. (ed.) *Teachers, Pupils and Primary Schooling: Continuity and Change*, London: Cassell.

Plate 1 Dome (Anon.)

Plate 2 Model toilets (Primary group, Chiswick)

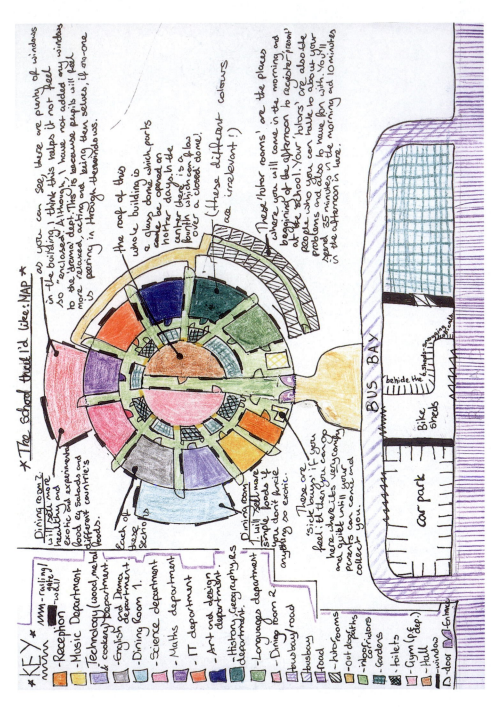

Plate 3 School I'd like: map (Rowan, 12, Hope Valley)

Plate 4 The sweet school (Rebecca, 8, Coventry)

Plate 5 School Plan (Ryan, 8, Bar Hill)

Plate 6 Environment school (Ben, upper secondary, Sutton)

Plate 7 School as a planet (Cara, 14, Winchester)

Plate 8 The school I'd like (Sarah, 11, Pickering)

Plate 9 The school I'd like (Duncan, secondary, Loughborough)

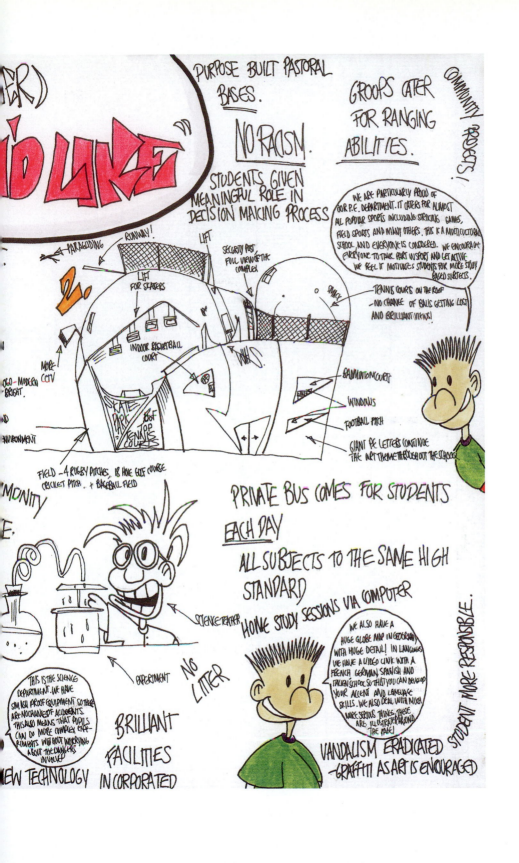

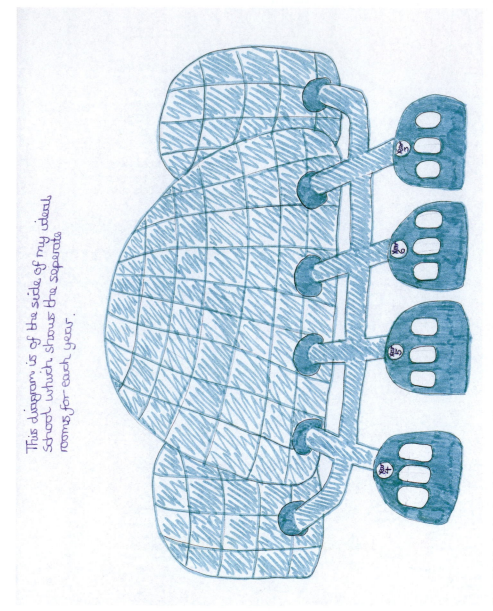

This diagram is of the side of my ideal school which shows the separate rooms for each year.

Plate 10 Ideal school and classrooms (Gemma, primary, Reading)

In presentation a computer would be programmed with all the researched information and visual aids enabling you to operate the robot from your seat and save embarrassment. The students would get to decorate the school after a unanimous vote. GCSE grades would be gained from your work through school, not a set of final exams.

I would like my school to be very futuristic, equipped with the most up-to-date facilities. School funding would not be a problem, lessons would be exciting and there would be no hand written work. Everything would be done by computers – writing what you think if it is relevant. There would be an inbuilt television into the wall which would automatically take notes from the programme being studied.

The rooms would be very light. Modern halogen lighting, and desk lamps for each student. There would be moulded seats to make you more comfortable and an inbuilt laptop in the desk for any research on the internet. Pupils would be able to take the class sometimes to specialise in certain areas.

The students would get a choice of the type of work they wanted to do. There would be no more than twelve students in a class to ensure all pupils receive optimum help. In class discussions there would be a screen for people to transfer their opinions onto and debate, choosing the most popular one. There would be no coursework or homework unless absolutely necessary.

Plate 11 'No more than 12 students in a class: all pupils receive optimum help' (Rachael, secondary, Amble)

Plate 12 'Here is a picture of my classroom' (Andrew, 8 Barr Hill)

Plate 13 My environmentally friendly school (Lucie, 10, Gloucester)

Plate 14 Volcano school (Patrick, primary, Romford)

Schaechter, J., Grosvenor, I. and Faust, A. (2000) '"I feel like I come from somewhere else". An examination of the way social exclusion impacts on African Caribbean pupils', *Education and Social Justice*, 3, 1, 9–16.

Smithers, R. (2002) 'Award winners praised for their passion', the *Guardian*, 28 October, 12.

Teacher Training Agency (2000) *Raising the Attainment of Minority Ethnic Pupils: Standards for the Award of Qualified Teacher Status*, London: TTA.

Weber, S. and Mitchell, C. (1995) *'That's Funny, You Don't Look Like a Teacher'*, London: Falmer Press.

Welch, G. and Mahoney, P. (2000) 'The teaching profession', in Docking, J. (ed.) *New Labour's Policies for Schools. Raising the Standard?*, London: David Fulton.

Woodward, W. (2002) 'Three year olds to grade teachers', the *Guardian*, 10 August, 1.

Younger, M. and Warrington, M. (1999) '"He's such a nice man, but he's so boring, you really have to make a conscious effort to learn": the views of Gemma, Daniel and their contemporaries on teacher quality and effectiveness', *Educational Review*, 51, 3, 231–41.

Teachers and special people

Teachers are kind.

Stephanie, 10, Sutton

〰〰

The only thing I like about going to school is P.E. and going to Bob [the school councillor] . . . I like going to Bob because I can draw and do whatever I like.

Robert, 12, Crewe

〰〰

My perfect teachers would have a very big smile, rosy cheeks and be kind to children. They would teach well and would be fun. They would let you go to the toilet whenever you want.

Ellis, 7, Glasgow

〰〰

One main thing that is important within a school is that the teachers are reliable. This means they turn up to lessons rather than arrange meetings or interviews for the relevant time. This is more important obviously if the subject is discussion based, and therefore more effort should be made to get to the lessons or send a supply teacher rather than instruct the class to write an article. This is more of a relevant aspect in my school as the sixth form is a consortium, so I have to travel by bus to four different sites. When teachers don't inform us of their absence it means that we end up in a different school, without the facilities that we are used to or able to use. However as a sixth form student I have realised that there is more to being a reliable teacher than just turning up to lessons. The teachers need to be prepared for questions that are raised rather than put the students off by saying they are unable to answer them. Teachers also need to adapt their teacher style if told by students that the way in which they teach is not actually teaching.

Diane, 18, Rushden

〰〰

English – Mr Write, Mrs Margin, Mrs Read, Graphics – Mr Sketch, Tech – Mr Create, Music – Mrs Viola, PE – Mr Fit, Mrs Jog, Maths – Mrs Multiple and Mr Minus, Art – Mr Picasso, Mrs Rosseti, Science – Mrs Explode, Mr Einstein, History – Mr Date and Mrs Fawkes, Geography – Mr Country.

Anna, 10, Derbyshire

The teachers would be easier to talk to, explain things a lot better and be experts in their field. I would like Linford Christie for P.E., Carol Vorderman for Maths, Tony Hart for Art, Bill Gates for I.T., Albert Einstein for Physics.

Matthew, 13, Bangor, Co. Down, N. Ireland

I would like to have a school that had really hard subjects, no strict teachers, a bigger play yard and field – bigger classrooms. I wish there was a couple more lessons than we already have. I wish there was no bullying. Bullying can be stopped by teachers putting bullies in detention and using a cane.

Amy, 9, North Shields

To make a good school I would say you need trust. Trust between a student and a teacher, between students, between teachers, and the whole school. You need fairness; teachers shouldn't show favouritism, they should keep it inside; and students should be expected to behave in lessons and get good treatment back. To make a good teacher you have to be fair by expecting the students to follow your rules and treating them fairly back.

You shouldn't blame people for things without any evidence e.g. no one has said a pupil's done something yet you suspect or don't like them, so blurt out what you think they've done, in front of another set of teachers or pupils.

If teachers have got favourite students they shouldn't show it by treating other students unfairly and maybe keeping favouritism to themselves or not obviously showing it.

The teachers should give their students a fair education and provide them with discipline and knowledge for older life.

Natasha, 12, Belper

All teachers should be:

Jolly
Have a sense of humour
Polite
Patient
Fair

Teachers should not mind if we have an opinion . . .

Kimberley, 11, Alfreton

The next fifteen years of this new century may see a fundamental change in the way the children are taught after 100 years of very little change. Why will this happen? It is because teachers, as we know them, may disappear. By this year, 2001, a quarter of all secondary school teachers are aged over fifty. By 2010 all of these will have retired and it may not be possible to replace them. Recruitment of graduates into a profession could dwindle to a trickle and teachers could be leaving in alarming numbers for more money and better working conditions outside. In the same period the opportunity to use information technology will grow, and successive governments may well decide to lose the battle of recruiting teachers and to pour money into computer technology instead.

The school I'd like is not like this at all. The school I'd like still has teachers and plenty of them. The school I'd like should still enable me to sit in a classroom with 25 other pupils and be able to debate with each other about the evilness of Lady Macbeth. It would allow me to mix magnesium and hydrochloric acid and hear the satisfying pop when I hold a lighted splint in the hydrogen gas produced. I should still be able to blow down a manometer for myself and test the pressure inside my lungs or use an acrylic heater to bend red acrylic into weird and wonderful shapes of desk tidies. Education is not just about importing information. Teachers enable complex experiments or risky activities to be supervised. The whole school environment helps children relate to adults and to learn how to treat elder generations and those with authority. It helps them to establish life and social skills, for example: respecting classmates' ideas, encouraging them to debate and listen to others' ideas with interest. This in turn allows us to develop our own ideas and theories about the world around us, rather than having to be 'spoon-fed' everything by distant information sources that are so far away we cannot relate to them. Teachers can add their own experiences and anecdotes, creating life in what can be boring subjects. They can answer specific questions, go over previous lessons or events that were not fully understood or topics if they have been forgotten.

Iona, 14, Winchester

❀❀❀

Who wants to be spoon-fed at a snail's pace? Who wants to be mentally or physically poked and prodded into an alert and responsive state of being by angry stupid teachers who are either there because they need a job to pay their mortgage and/or enjoyed their own schooldays so much they want to spend all their adult lives in school too? What sort of person becomes a teacher, acquires that horrid habitual authoritative tone in their voice, expects total obedience from gambolling foals and rough and tumbling lion cubs, would suppress the energy and expressiveness and articulateness of naive youngsters and try to instil silence, conformity and a rather academic orientation on all their captives?

I don't understand why teachers ask so many questions. It seems to me that it is the learner that should ask the questions. Give us the freedom to ask questions and do us the courtesy of helping us find answers.

Hero Joy, 14, home educated, Kent

❀❀❀

Teachers should be under 49.

Sophie, 9, Richmond on Thames

❀❀❀

Rightly or wrongly, the power relationships between pupils and teachers are unequal in most schools, but I think that teachers frequently abuse their authority. It is often seen as acceptable for the young to be treated with disrespect, or to be humiliated. There is a very pronounced 'respect double standard' in schools, which manifests itself in the way pupils are spoken to ... A 'ticking off' tends to have more to do with power and punishment than with logic or negotiation ... Many of the ritualised details of school are degrading and unnecessary. For instance, it is quite common for a teacher to insist that a class stand up in his/her presence, until he/she has the condescension to allow them to sit! Teachers are addressed by titles, rather than first names – some even insist on being called 'sir'. I can see no benefit in this outdated habit. In general, pupils are expected to be deferent, while teachers are allowed to be unpleasant, high-handed and often unreasonable.

Lorna, 14, Ipswich

∽∽∽∽

I think teachers shouldn't be called Mrs or Mr they should be called by nick-names (nice nicknames) – or even called by their first names. My main reason for thinking this is because then our teachers would seem like real people and not monsters who stand at the front of the classroom shouting orders at us! Teachers should add enjoyment to a lesson!

Hannah, 13, Ammanford

∽∽∽∽

Our last topic is about what some people call teachers but to us are creatures that give us truckfulls of homework and make our lives a living nightmare! We would like teachers that understand children and teenagers because there have been countless events where I have been told that my teacher does not understand me or the way I think which is a main quality to have if you want to be a teacher. We would also like teachers that do not shout but simply ask in a polite manner for us not to speak as loudly because 99.9% of the time all I hear is: SHUT UP which usually makes us louder. We would appreciate teachers that co-operate and say things that we understand for instance if a teacher asks you 'Who do you think you're talking to'. If you don't answer you'll be accused of ignoring them but if you do answer you'll be accused of being cheeky and answering back. It's a no win situation that they put you in.

Anon., lower secondary, Bristol

∽∽∽∽

I believe that school should teach in an exciting way because when children learn and have fun, they take more in.

Andrew, 10, Cardiff

∽∽∽∽

I think the teachers should be over 25 at least because the younger ones don't have as much control over the class. I think there should be more teachers on duty like around the tennis courts at lunch because you get people smoking and there are loads of sights.

Oliver, 11, Reading

∽∽∽∽

Everyone would like their teachers to be funny, kind and happy, not bossy, angry or nasty.

> Zoe, Sam, Fiona, Jayne and Kirsty, Special School, Upton, Cheshire

The teachers will be fresh out of college and so they will remember what school is like and so they will know the hardships that we go through and so will take pity on us and they will be easy going and teach us in a fun calming sort of way.

> Edward, 14, Loughborough

I think teachers should be a little bit barmy and dance and not just sit down and drink tea & coffee.

> Kirsty, 10, Cardiff

I would like all the teachers to be male and female so that we have a mixture of both. I would want a female head teacher as I find male head teachers a bit scary if you are going to be told off.

I would like to have older teachers, preferably in their late 20s and early 30s. This is because I like teachers with lots of experience and older teachers have more time in their lives to learn about things to tell us. I would also like an election each year for which teacher each class will have. Each class will vote for the teacher they want and if there is a draw it is the first name out of the hat.

It really is important that teachers are happy because if they are not, they are not very nice to the rest of the class . . .

The school I'd like would be very rich . . . this would mean that teachers got good pay and might teach better.

> Sarah, 9, Sheffield

I think we should have a 'teach the teacher' day. We can teach the teacher how it feels to be a kid and see how hard and fast we have to do our work and so WE can set the standard.

> Jonathan, 10, Cardiff

We would only have the teachers who knew and understood what they were talking about; they would all be passionate about their subjects and help us to unleash our passions.

> Maisie, 14, London

I would like teachers that are not so up tight and are sorry a lot of the time. Also I would like it if we were all given our own amount of time needed to do work. This would help a teacher see a class of individuals rather than just a class of kids. This would also create a more calm and suitable situation for children and teachers.

> Evan, 12, Loughborough

School is the mould, which shapes our future. It is where we spend the most valuable time of our life – childhood. Yet I know from first hand experience that many aspects should be changed: the cold and impersonal attitude of teachers who drive for results, results, results, instead of creating happy memories and valuable life experience for young people.

These young people, far from being 'an empty pot ready to be filled full of know-ledge' are simply a locked case, their potential to be released by careful nurturing and gentle encouragement from a caring teacher. Teachers should not be tied down by the tight restrictions the curriculum presents. They should be able to plan a lesson the way they wish and develop it into a worthwhile life lesson; maybe the pupils will treasure and apply within their lives. Captivation of imagination guarantees a lesson will stay with a person and not be forgotten the moment the classroom is vacated. In many ways I feel that to certain teachers, teaching has lost its wonder and the sense of fulfilment that comes from passing your knowledge on.

This is the point I believe that they should stop teaching. If these teachers no longer have enthusiasm for the subjects they teach and the words they say have lost their meaning, then children will not gain the knowledge they need from them. The way to tell a good teacher is that they make you want to listen and get involved in the lesson, not to be forever looking at the clock bored out of your mind waiting to leave.

Angela, 15, Croydon

∽∽∽

What I would change about the teachers is the way they are paid. I would make it that the teachers would only get paid if the pupils thought they were teaching properly. Some teachers don't explain things properly and if you say you don't under-stand, they say you haven't been paying attention. By the time of exams you don't know some of the stuff you are being tested on and then you end up failing your exam, just because the teacher didn't take the time to explain something to you. They shouldn't be allowed to ask pupils personal questions like why they were off, as it is none of their business. It is only the business of the school office, your register teacher, and yourself. They shouldn't pick on certain pupils just because the teacher doesn't like them or if they know the pupil doesn't like the teacher. They should always be on their feet helping pupils unless they are marking jotters and the pupils are out at the teacher's desk, and they should never focus all their attention on one pupil; it should be equal for everyone.

Lindsay, lower secondary, Renfrew

∽∽∽

The teachers can tell us what they think of us, but in a Dream school we could tell the teachers what we think of them. So we could write them reports, and give them good or bad marks. Wouldn't it be nice if we could choose which teacher we wanted for every subject. That would mean the teachers would have to work extra hard to be perfect at every subject.

Alice and Prema, 8, Birmingham

∽∽∽

I would like a few teachers that listen and understand my point of view. I would also like teachers who are calm. The school would have a respectable head teacher who listened and took control. He would be responsible for making sure everybody enjoyed themselves and were happy.

Emily, 11, Birmingham

∽∾∽

The teachers would have to speak in rhyme. When you've been naughty, the teachers can't tell you off straight away, as they have to think of something that will rhyme . . .

Bethany, 13, Ipswich

∽∾∽

Every teacher should be able to decorate and bring in their own personalities into their classrooms, that way the teacher might feel more relaxed and at ease, and if the teachers are relaxed then so are the pupils.

Sam, 14, Penryn

∽∾∽

Teachers is another big problem at my school, but even though I hate them, and they are so strict and terrifyingly horrible I would like to keep them the same way they are now. This may seem weird because what I have said previously in this essay, but my school gets its good results because of this strictness we have in classrooms. If I said I wanted easy going teachers who all wanted a good laugh, I would not learn very much at all. I'm quite intelligent for my age at the moment because of my teachers and how they are. Education would not be the same without the teachers being how they are at the moment. Education is about preparing me for the outside world and how to work and socialise in it. If I did not have those teachers I would go out in the world not prepared and would receive bad results. So I would keep the teachers the same.

Scott, 14, Romford

∽∾∽

Please pay our teachers whatever you need to keep them in the profession. They really are the most precious resource we have and must stay part of the schools of the future.

D. McC, primary, Belfast

∽∾∽

Many people think school should have no teachers but that would not be a school. Because I spent a lot of time in junior school I am now behind on lots of work and if the teachers did not help me I would not know a lot at all. I do not like to be silly in lessons, and other people are being silly because I think we should learn and get good G.C.S.E. results. I think my ideal school would be to put bad behaved people in a small cubicle and a teacher to watch them. At least then we will all be able to get our work done. School is to learn not to be stupid. 2001 should be a new start for us.

Laura, 12, Bideford

∽∾∽

Some of our teachers get very tired and I think that we should give them a break and let our parents have a go at teaching because my mum always says she would be a good teacher.

Sam, 10, Cardiff

∽∽∽∽

I do not believe in the ability of OFSTED to make an accurate and fair examination of a school. Therefore I would start a new inspection system. Again, I believe it would be important to rename this 'Teaching Support', due to the changed nature of the system I would put in place. I would have an expert in each subject area as a 'helper', and they must be a qualified teacher. The teaching support would not just last a week, it could last as long as is needed ... The assessment would not be based on the rigid criteria of OFSTED, in fact there would be no assessment, but only advice based on the methods used. This done, the helpers would highlight any area where the individual teachers needed to improve, and stay and help until these goals had been achieved.

Robin, 17

∽∽∽∽

When teachers apply for jobs their qualifications are looked at closely. Just because they are clever and have good grades, it doesn't necessarily mean they will be a good teacher. I think teachers should be tested on how well they teach a class during their interview for a teaching post, it would solve a lot of problems!

Anon., 12, Bristol

∽∽∽∽

The teachers are all nice but when the children are bored the teachers get cross.

Amber, 5, Oxford

∽∽∽∽

I would like more teachers so it would be easier for all the other teachers.

Lauren, 6, Barnsley

∽∽∽∽

My dream school will have a plan – your own weekly plan and experts that can come to your school. Lockers for the teachers to put their stuff and a BIG lounge for the teachers and a teachers' bed so they can relax when they need to.

Marikka, 8, Norwich

∽∽∽∽

I think that the teachers should be allowed to bring their dogs to school. They could sit and walk around in the classroom in lessons and give it a comfy feel. Also, stroking dogs lowers blood pressure!

Melanie, 12, Ammanford

∽∽∽∽

My dream school has silver classrooms. It is a weird school but it is cool! There are no teachers, we learn ourselves.

Thomas, 8, Oxford

Part 3

Staying power

Craig.obrien

The school I'd like

A a B b C c D d E e F f G g H h I i J j K k L l M m N n O o P p Q q R r S s T t U u W

Maths

Literacy

SCIENCE

HISTORY   ART

1 2 3 4 5 6 7 8 9 10

12
11 1 2 3
10   4
9   5
8 7 6

Tuesday July 28th
Once upon a time there
Lived a little girl
called essa
She went on
the field Playing
Skiping ropes

2 x 2 = 4
6 x 1 = 6
12 x 2 = 24

headmasters
office

Knock
Before
enter

Puma

Purabada Nike

CB
Swim
Bag

PEBI
Amax

food
Cola

Chapter 7

Identities and equalities

'I resented being told what to wear, what to think, what to believe, what to say and when to say it'

Social historians of the industrialised world have documented the powerful effects of the introduction of compulsory schooling on the institutionalisation of childhood. School became a designated site of childhood, a space organised and controlled by adults to aid an ordered transition from childhood to adulthood. This process of institutionalisation was also shaped by the emergence and adoption of psychological theories, professional knowledge and practices which defined 'childhood' and, in turn, established 'accepted' educational and social development phases. Children's school lives became hierarchically structured according to age and ability (Woodhead, 1997; Baker, 2001). Further, conditions and practices emerged in schools which had as their object the normalisation of behaviour through the production of self-disciplined individuals who adhered to 'explicit and implicit rules of conduct and norms of conscience as if they were their own'. These normative practices acted as moral regulation – personal identities were disciplined and shaped through the self-appropriation of ideas about what was 'right and wrong, possible and impossible, normal and pathological' (Rousmaniere, Dehli and de Coninck-Smith, 1997: 3, 5). In short, the introduction of compulsory schooling resulted in childhood being spatially compartmentalised, and children's lives and identities being increasingly regulated and shaped by the interior life of the school. Individual children could be judged according to their degree of fit with prevailing theorisations and, at the same time, in order to participate in adult–child encounters in school, children had to become aware of the normative regime of expectations. However, the production of the self-governing human subject through pedagogical practices and discourses also involved children in acts of negotiation, subversion and resistance.

Research on late-twentieth-century schooling and identity formation in childhood and adolescence indicates the continuing relevance of this historical analysis for understanding the interiority of schools. Identities continue to be regulated and shaped by institutional procedures, practices and discourses. For example, James *et al.* have described how temporal and spatial control functioning through the curriculum significantly shapes a child's 'educational identity' as either 'success' or 'failure' (James, Jenks and Prout, 1998). Mac an Ghaill (1988) and Gillborn (1990) have documented the operation of racialised teacher discourse and practices in English schools and pupil resistance. Armstrong (1999) has explored how school discourses routinely collapse individual identities into stereotypes and categories. The individual becomes the category – 'ethnic minority' or 'special needs' or 'she's free meals' or 'bottom set' – and as a consequence occupies certain social spaces determined by these categories. Regulation and resistance are powerful themes in current educational research. The concern of researchers with documenting pupil resistance also parallels a shift in conceptual frames in childhood studies away from socialisation (becoming) towards an increasing emphasis on the child as an individual social actor (being). Indeed, some researchers working within this frame have been able to document how the social order of English schools has changed and that children are now expected to exercise greater self-responsibility and autonomy in their lived school experience (Brannen, Hepstinstall and Bhopal, 2000). What, then, of the understanding that schoolchildren have of these processes of institutionalisation and individualisation and how they impact on their identity?

The evidence in the 'School I'd Like' archive suggests that children are very aware of how schools and their attendant social practices operate to produce normalised behaviour and social citizens:

> Schooling is a process, taking in the many square, hexagonal and octagonal pegs and cutting off eccentricities to leave bare, uniform round pegs.

Children also recognise that certain 'person qualities' are described, defined and enacted within the normative regime of the school and resent this process:

> In my ideal school the whole philosophy that dominates schools now will be dropped ... We will no longer be treated like herds of an identical animal waiting to be civilised before we are let loose on the world. It will be recognised that it is our world too ... There will be no ridiculous hierarchy who don't even know us, to whom we are constantly proving ourselves.

> ... children are the underclass, so low in status that they are not worth listening to ... [and the] curriculum ... is concerned with efficiency, rather than fulfilment. It prioritises the preparation of a useful workforce, and makes little allowance for individual preference and talent.

Children resented the idea of 'one-size fits all'. Norms of performance were condemned as damaging to self-esteem and, thereby, individual identity: 'I don't like the way children are expected to do this by seven and that by eleven' and:

> results are not comparable between two people; they are worthy as their own entities ... Encouraging this attitude and discouraging marks and ranking will increase everybody's feeling of self-worth.

As with all areas of concern raised by the children, criticism was balanced by practical suggestions for changing the social order of schools:

> There will be adults who like young people there to help us discover things. They will be friends and co-workers to pupils and will be called by their first names even though they are older.

Schools would be run by the 'whole learning community', they would work to promote an 'atmosphere of cohesion and unity, avoiding segregation where poss-ible'. Students would learn at their own pace, schools would 'acknowledge . . . differ-ing circumstances', 'all people would be valued' and no one would be expected 'to be the same'. Schools would be sites of 'harmony' where everyone, irrespective of their background, would be welcome.

This vision of the welcoming, valuing and inclusive school accords with the find-ings of more broadly framed studies where a small, but growing number of researchers have attempted to ascertain young people's hopes and fears for the future. However, the evident desire for a world more inclusive of difference is matched by a strong sense of negativity, helplessness, and fear about the anticipated problems facing the world (see, for example, Holden, 1989; Hutchinson, 1996; Nurmi, 1997; Hicks and Slaughter, 1998; Eckersley, 1999).

Despondency with the project of normalising and the need for change is also very much in evidence in Blishen's collection as the following extracts testify:

> Churn, churn, churn . . . a stuffed puppet . . . too apathetic to think, . . . too lethargic to do . . . I have felt continually suppressed at school . . .

> . . . coming last has no stigma attached to it . . . pupils are not streamed graded, since groups will form naturally . . . This 'grouping' does not give rise to envy or branding because it is not imposed by adults.

> Teachers would be there to help and not to organize . . . When I'm older I'll establish this place for people who feel different.

> The pupils would also be treated as individuals and not as a flock of sheep all with the same purpose in life . . . The pupils would be of all nationalities and creeds: boys and girls, Jews and Moslems. This would help them in later life to have no colour preju-dice and to know that one nationality or creed is no better than another.

> Children should be given equal rights . . . equal attention should be given to all . . .

> Each morning, for the minimum of four years, a young sensitive person becomes part of a system which cannot accept him as an individual. Teachers dismiss individual actions as a calamitous breach of school regulations. This person is then accepted as an unequal. Rejected and observed with guarded curiosity . . . [as one] who is attempting to endanger the security of their society . . . His whole system is discor-dant with the system he is obliged to accept. Eventually the one is forced to accept the ruling of the majority.
>
> (Blishen, 1969: 21–2, 35–7, 79, 135)

A very strong link across the two sets of data is concern with what Blishen termed 'a sore point' – school uniform (Blishen, 1969: 145–8). The imposition of school uniform was for many children an affront to individuality, a determination to produce 'superficial sameness'. Where children accepted that a uniform was a lev-eller, they invariably also produced drawings and new designs to make what was 'outdated' more tolerable.

Children in the 1960s and in the opening decade of the new millennium saw themselves very much as social actors confronted by a closed social order in school. There are examples in both sets of data of children acting as advocates for those perceived by both the system and, by implication, by the children themselves, as being unfairly treated and less able to speak out. Occasionally, there are poignant statements from those who felt themselves to be both different and outsiders:

> Each child ... would be regulated with a visor, which would act as a screen, as well as a pocket modem ... if you were shy of your appearance, you could create your own virtual body or scan a picture of yourself into it. Your classmates and peers would then see you as that virtual image.

Such moments act as a valuable reminder of the need for researchers and analysts in thinking about young people's identities and the ways they deploy the resources at their disposal in these settings to pay close attention to how young people represent their lived experiences, their lives as lived and enacted in educational settings, and to recognise that their identities emerge in 'conditions not of their own choosing' (Epstein, 2002: 149).

Is it possible for schools as institutions to offer young people the type of conditions that match their demands for inclusiveness, equality and justice? School reform in England has placed 'performance' at the centre of school effectiveness. Michael Fielding, in a challenging critique of the seductive model of the 'effective and performing' school, developed a typology of school organisational orientation. Schools could be seen as:

- impersonal organisations – 'mechanistic organizations primarily concerned with efficiency.'
- sentimental communities – 'self indulgent in the sense that its concern for persons and for the wider dimensions of human achievement are over-stated and under-realized, often leading to a complacency and self-regard that obstructs rather than enhances ... learning.'
- high performance organizations – 'here community is valued, but primarily for instrumental purposes within the context of the market place.'
- person-centred communities – 'teachers operating within the person-centred framework typically take the view that teaching subjects or getting results is only justifiable if it does actually help students to become better persons.'

Performativity, for Fielding, was 'intellectually shallow', 'spiritually destitute' and a 'betrayal of education'. The person-centred school offered a compelling alternative to other organisational models, as it retained a commitment to achieving desirable results, but in ways which were more creative and 'more explicit, more ... understanding of how we become persons' (Fielding, 2000: 51–4). What model would be chosen by the child who ended their consideration of the school of the future with 'a note to all you adults'?

You know what it's like to be a child in secondary school so please next time you nag shout or embarrass a child or pupil think back to your days at school and appreciate how we cope.

Anon., 11–13, Bristol

Further reading

Armstrong, F. (1999) 'Inclusion, curriculum and the struggle for space in school', *International Journal of Inclusive Education*, 3, 1, 75–87.

Baker, B.M. (2001) *In Perpetual Motion. Theories of Power, Educational History, and the Child*, New York, NY: Peter Lang.

Brannen, J., Hepstinstall, E. and Bhopal, K. (2000) *Connecting Children: Care and Family Life in Later Childhood*, London: Routledge.

Eckersley, R. (1999) 'Dreams and expectations: young people's expected and preferred futures and their significance for education', *Futures*, 31, 73–90.

Epstein, D. (2002) 'Re-theorising friendship in educational settings', *Discourse: Studies in the Cultural Politics of Education*, 23, 2, 149–51.

Fielding, M. (2000) 'The person-centred School', *Forum*, 42, 2, 51–4.

Gillborn, D. (1990) *'Race', Ethnicity and Education*, London: Unwin Hyman.

Hicks, D. and Slaughter, R. (eds) (1998) *Futures Education: The World Yearbook of Education, 1998*, London: Kogan Page.

Holden, C. (1989) 'Teaching about the future with younger children', in Slaughter, R. (ed.) *Studying the Future: An Introductory Reader*, Canberra: Commission for the Future and Bicentennial Authority.

Hutchinson, F. (1996) *Educating Beyond Violent Futures*, London: Routledge.

James, A., Jenks, C. and Prout, A. (1998) *Theorizing Childhood*, Cambridge: Polity Press.

Mac an Ghaill, M. (1988) *Young, Gifted and Black: Student–Teacher Relations in the Schooling of Black Youth*, Milton Keynes: Open University Press.

Nurmi, J.-E. (1997) 'Self definition and mental health during adolescence and young adulthood', in Schulenberg, J., Maggs, J. and Hurrelmann, K. (eds) *Health Risks and Developmental Trajectories During Adolescence*, Cambridge, MA: Harvard University Press.

Rousmaniere, K., Dehli, K. and de Conick-Smith, N. (1997) *Discipline, Moral Regulation, and Schooling*, New York, NY: Garland.

Woodhead, M. (1997) 'Psychology and the cultural construction of children's needs', in James, A. and Prout, A. (eds) *Constructing and Reconstructing Childhood: Contemporary Issues in the Sociological Study of Childhood*, London: Falmer Press.

Identities and equalities

I left school last year at the age of thirteen, and enrolled at a local college
… I left because I felt that the regime was oppressive and, like most oppressive
regimes, coercive and difficult to change. I resented being told what to wear, what to
think, what to believe, what to say and when to say it. In the average school, the children are the underclass, so low in status that they are not worth listening to.

In the present state system, there is a set curriculum that is concerned with efficiency, rather than fulfilment. It prioritises the preparation of a useful workforce, and
makes little allowance for individual preference and talent.

I think that school uniforms are both degrading and unnecessary. They violate the
individual's right of self-expression. Some argue that uniforms create a sense of equality between students, regardless of social background, but I would dispute this.
Firstly, it doesn't work. Children, like adults, are acutely aware of their differences,
and it is naïve to propose that class inequality can be eliminated by identical clothing.
Secondly, the object should be to promote tolerance, not sameness. There is nothing
wrong with people understanding each other's differences. There is nothing wrong
with different groups forming their own identities. For superficial sameness to be
imposed on one group by another *is* wrong.

The school I'd like would stand for freedom, tolerance and flexibility. The school
would be run by the whole learning community. Members of the community would
support and respect each other, and nobody would be victimised or humiliated.
There would be an atmosphere of cohesion and unity, avoiding segregation where
possible. Students would be able to learn at their own pace, the school acknowledging their differing circumstances. All people would be valued, and enabled to develop
their own abilities to the full, whether these are practical, academic, social, physical
or artistic. It would be a place where students of all ages came voluntarily, because
they actually wanted to be there.

Lorna, 14, Ipswich

∽∽∽

… treat us all as ourselves, not expect us to be the same or be able to do the
same things.

Kimberley, 11, Alfreton

∽∽∽

**I would like a school which influences young people in becoming respons-
ible adults** … I would like a lively, happy but varied school where every subject is
taken seriously but enjoyed to the last second … and I would love a school where
people respect and accept others for who they are no matter what! Why is this so
simple yet so hard to achieve?!!

Susan, 16, Llangollen

∽∽∽

My ideal school would be where everyone can be equal. There would be no
bullying, no racism and no division by intelligence, abilities or sex. There would be more
involvement in the layout and facilities by the pupils' opinion and what the pupils want.

Philip, 12, Loughborough

∽∽∽

My school would be one where people were treated much more qualitatively and much less quantitatively. This cannot be enforced, but can rise from logical analysis and observation of humans. It is the normal way for human interaction to take place and is best done through things like art and music. The 'results' are not comparable between two people; they are worthy as their own entities and good in their own right. Encouraging this attitude and discouraging marks and ranking will increase everybody's feeling of self-worth and from that achievement of their very best.

Jonathan, 17, Manchester

ഗ്ഗ

I am ill qualified to speak of schools since I don't attend one but ... it doesn't stop me dreaming about school and it perhaps gives me a different perspective from many other children my age.

So what would my ideal school be like? Apart from, quite obviously, being inclusive? The word comprehensive springs to mind, a neighbourhood school that is comprehensive in what it offers, a school for anyone, brainy or barmy, a techno-whizz, arty-farty fandango of a place. There is a sense of the local community investing its money and its hopes and its time in me and my contemporaries, of children being cherished and valued.

What's special about a child? We know every child is special and irreplaceable and precious to at least its own family, but children are different from adults, right? They haven't learned to take responsibility for themselves and others, haven't learned to control their impulsivity and to think before they leap ... we also have awfully rapid metabolisms compared with the old fogies running the ship and soak up new information like some archaic device called blotting paper. We're the future rulers of the world, the future hands and cannon fodder. We're the people you must entrust your dreams to in order that they might be brought to fruition. And damn it all, we also are the young upstarts with our own ideas, who seem to take a perverse delight in revelling in our youth, our energy and in shocking our elders and betters with innovative lifestyles and flights of fancy. Each of us, to begin with, is an unknown quantity, an unfolding personality that presented with this or that opportunity may veer towards brilliance or off the rails altogether.

Hero Joy, home educated, 14, Kent

ഗ്ഗ

School should have Muslim prayers because in our school we have Jewish prayers and Christian assembly and we think it would be nice to have Muslim prayers because those who are little Muslim children should learn more about their religion.

Anisha and Ayesha, 12 and 13, Bury

ഗ്ഗ

My ideal school would be one where all races worked together in harmony, so there would have to be a prayer room that would have everything they need for worship. It would have a separate area for every religion under the sun and could be used at any time, whether the person just wanted to relax or had something very important to pray about.

Primary class, 9–11, Oldham

ഗ്ഗ

My ideal school will be open to everyone, people from all over the world, people from every hamlet, village, town, city, country and continent will be welcomed with warm arms. Every black, white, mixed-raced, Indian, African, Jamaican, Canadian and Cuban girl and boy will walk around my school without fear of others. Every different race and sex and disabled people will play with each other with laughter and joy, without care of each others differences. People will enjoy their uniqueness and will enjoy others too. The whole school will celebrate and enjoy other religion's festivals. There will be no uniform, for there would be no need. Everybody will respect each other's clothes and how they dress. In the mornings the children will do important lessons such as, English, mathematics, history and science. And then in the afternoon the children will get a choice of fun activities like art, sports, IT, drama, music or going on a trip to find out something interesting like what environment pill bugs like best. One day a week the afternoon activity choice would be R.E, trying to find out about other peoples' cultures and beliefs so that they know what other people in this school believe in when they celebrate so that even if they are different cultures a Muslim will say merry Christmas to a Christian and be able to understand what sorts of activities they do over this time. They could also go to a geography lesson and find out about different places and where others in this school come from and what changes those who have come to this school from different countries have had when moving to England. Everybody who has religion in my school will have a two-week holiday twice a year on the most important celebrations to their religion. If they have no religion then they may have Christian holidays (Easter and Christmas). The reason that I say my school *will* and instead of my school *would* is because I do believe that such a school can exist.

Millie, 11, Bristol

〰〰〰

In my ideal school it would be made clear to all pupils that they would all be treated as equal citizens. No-one would be turned away because they were black or because they lived in a caravan. This is deeply unfair and, I feel, cruel.

Elizabeth, lower secondary, Leiston

〰〰〰

What I would change about the atmosphere is that no one should be picked on or slagged just because they are different from everyone else, or if they wear different clothes. Everyone should treat other people the way they would like to be treated, and if someone didn't like someone else they shouldn't call them names or slag them, they should just say nothing.

Lindsay, lower secondary, Renfrew

〰〰〰

I hate it when teachers go on about how bullying is wrong and should be 'stamped out in our school'. This is true, bullying is wrong but people don't realise that actually teachers bully children more than you may think! I've heard teachers say to pupils when they've done good work, 'this is far too good for *you*!'. This is terrible and teachers should work hard to respect everyone's abilities and disabilities equally in their classes.

Rowan, 12, Hope Valley

〰〰〰

In my ideal school the whole philosophy that dominates schools now will be dropped. It will be somewhere thriving with different personalities and gifts, where these things can be developed and used to help everyone else. We will no longer be treated like herds of an identical animal waiting to be civilised before we are let loose on the world. It will be recognised that it is our world too. There will be adults who like young people there to help us discover things. They will be friends and co-workers to pupils and will be called by their first names even though they are older. The authority they will have will be based on moral leverage: they can per-suade pupils to do the right thing. However, where there is no moral leverage, petty power games will be recognised as pointless. No more comments like 'Andrew, did I ask you to stand up? Hm? No. I suggest you sit back down immediately. We've still got a good minute until the bell rings,' will be overheard as soon as some poor chap who's too tall for his flimsy chair half raises himself to stretch.

There will be no ridiculous hierarchy who don't even know us, to whom we are constantly proving ourselves. Exams will not exist, and neither will a one-size-fits-all curriculum. My ideal school will produce real people who respect and accommodate others instead of having prejudices. No one will have unfair power over them and so they will never abuse their power over others as so many adults do today. They will have been treated fairly and celebrated as individuals; not discriminated against just because they are powerless and a generation younger than the people in charge. Because they will have been encouraged instead of being restrained, they will develop into creative, assertive people who will work together with their individual talents to rebuild the earth.

Miriam, 15, Reading

∞∞∞∞

The disabled facilities would be best and would have easy access all around the school. The school would be a good place for disabled and non-disabled students because of the facilities. Also it would be safe and welcoming.

Megan, 13, Warminster

∞∞∞∞

Pupils often have a negative attitude towards the staff room & what goes on in there. If they sometimes get a peek and see biscuits etc. ... being handed around, they think it is unfair. I think a good way to solve this problem is to have a place where pupils can talk & listen to music, and perhaps have a little food. They just need somewhere they can relax at breaks. I would have this in my school because it would please the pupils and isn't very much trouble.

Hannah, 14, Ipswich

∞∞∞∞

My school would welcome children of all different types of disabilities so that lots of fortunate people around them could understand how it feels for them. This would encourage people to be more respectful for others, whether it's for their feelings, or property. There will also be no bullying tolerated. I wasn't bullied but someone (I won't say who), said 'OH! Shut up you deaf girl'. If pupils do any of these things, it will upset those with disabilities, and may be so much that it might put them off something for life ...

Alice, 12, Croydon

∞∞∞∞

Instead of pupils having either packed lunch, money or free school meals, everyone would have a ticket with the same amount of money on it that way everybody would be equal.

Sam, 14, Penryn

⌇⌇⌇⌇

In my perfect school there would still be rules but they would guide us, not confine us ... there would still be punishments but these punishments would matter to the student. They would have to miss their favourite lesson for a week and have to take a double lesson of their worst subjects instead. Teachers and pupils would be equals, no privileges and disadvantages, everybody would be in the same boat ... We would not be concerned about whether we did the best in class, but only about whether everyone was happy with what he or she was doing and how he or she was progressing.

Maisie, 13, London

⌇⌇⌇⌇

I find with the condition I have known as Dyslexia, I am at a disadvantage from the start compared with normal children. I take twice as long to read the questions and have the same time to finish the exam as any other pupil ... but with help or more time I would have improved my marks.

Anon., 12, Bristol

⌇⌇⌇⌇

... I would like ... female and male nurses on hand for privacy and so they can have personal chats about growing up.

Sarah, 11, Cardiff

⌇⌇⌇⌇

My dream school would be one that could offer all students comfort, security, friendship and a fun and interesting education. I would also have smaller classes so that the teachers got to know you as a person, not just another pupil, and you would have more of their time and attention.

Children nowadays quite often feel that they have the right to be very cruel and excluding of others. I feel it is particularly strong in my age group of girls between 11 and 16. Perhaps if there were more supervision and intervention by teachers fewer people would suffer the pain that comes from being treated badly.

Sarah, 13, Guildford

⌇⌇⌇⌇

The process of virtual education is a simple system. Each child in Britain would be regulated with a visor, which would act as a screen, as well as a pocket modem ... The visor would act as a portal or window to your virtual body, and you would see through its eyes, viewing a virtual recreation of a classroom and equipment. The ingenious aspect of it would be that if you were shy of your appearance, you could create your own virtual body or scan a picture of yourself into it. Your classmates and peers would then see you as that virtual image.

Andrew, 14, Stoke Golding

⌇⌇⌇⌇

To improve my hearing problem, I would like a special microphone where you would switch hearing-aids to a 'T'. (They have these in churches.) This would be useful for assemblies, as I often get too embarrassed to give the transmitter to the Head Teacher because people in the school wouldn't know what it was and might get the wrong impressions. This way, I wouldn't worry about anyone asking if I can hear every five minutes.

Alice, 12, Croydon

⋙⋘

The school is as big as the solar system and the evening is good. Everyone has their own mug with their name on it and we have our own laptops.

Ben, 7, Coventry

⋙⋘

I think differences make the world go round, kids need to know that. They need to learn that more than 'the rotation of the earth' in science! I think schools must teach differences and celebrate them. At the moment schools do the opposite, trying to make everybody normal. Take the idea of the school uniform, I think they are taking away kids' background and identity and makes school a colourless and boring place. The worst thing about uniform is making all children look the same. In my dream school there will NOT be any uniform!

Kate, London[1]

⋙⋘

My dream school would be where children are treated with respect. Children and teachers would think of each other as equals. Children are taught not to criticise or bully others, who are different from themselves. One of the most important things about my dream school, it would have no racist or sexist abuse to other students. So no one had to feel like an outcast. I don't think pupils should have to wear uniforms, as everyone is different. My ideal school would let you dye your hair and wear earrings and rings.

Megan, 13, Warminster

⋙⋘

There should be no school uniform and no rules about what hairstyles we have etc. This would not affect how we work and would make us happier, meaning that we would like school better and be more likely to come.

David, 13, Reading

⋙⋘

There should be no uniform as these take away individuality and free expression.

Philip, 13, Loughborough

⋙⋘

1 (Note from Kate's mum) Kate hasn't been to school since December 2000 as she hated it so much – it definitely wasn't the school she'd like! Kate doesn't really care about the prize, more an acknowledgement that she is a capable writer when the school had claimed she couldn't do English GCSE because she couldn't physically write with her hands or talk with her mouth (she is a communication aid user).

Children should wear what they want to. With school uniform nobody looks different. We all look the same. We should all look unique.

Katie, 10, Cardiff

〰〰〰

Lets face it. Barely anybody actually likes school uniform. Now I don't think there should be one. Answer me, what does it do for anyone? It just makes us all look the same, not allowing us to show our individual qualities in the way we like to dress.

Melanie, 12, Ammanford

〰〰〰

I would have a school uniform designed by pupils or no uniform at all … I don't have to give much evidence to support no uniforms all you have look at is the results in schools in Belgium, or the Netherlands. People will argue that children will envy other people for wearing a different item of clothing. From my opinion that idea is ludicrous. For a start we live in a democratic society we are surely meant to be acting in the best interests of the children. With myself being a child I know what the children want (no uniform). Also people go on about children 'stepping out of line' well why do we have the highest vandalism in Europe?

Alexander, lower secondary, Kidlington

〰〰〰

We should be able to wear what we want to show off what we believe in.

Jack, 10, Cardiff

〰〰〰

I think uniforms are a good thing they make a school look smart and you feel good in a uniform and everyone is the same.

Josh, 10, Belmont

〰〰〰

Also I would keep the uniforms so that we can feel that we belong somewhere.

Sam, 14, Penryn

〰〰〰

School Uniform
*   Avoids bullying
*   Shows an immediate difference between home and school
*   Identification
*   Uncomfortable
*   Too strict
*   More options.

Overall, I think school uniform is a good thing, but some aspects should be changed to adapt to the future. In our school we have recently had a change to our uniform. Girls are now allowed to wear trousers. It is a change for the better. We have to wear ties and blazers until we get into year 10, then we wear jumpers. Everyone I know hates wearing a blazer because they are really uncomfortable and annoying. It would be better to wear a jumper from year 7.

Anon., lower secondary, Bristol

〰〰〰

Why be smart when you can be bold,
School uniform should be cool and groovy,
Not boring and old.
Bright colours like fluorescent yellow and green
Stand out on trips,
Make your school be seen!
The buildings,
Aha! The red and grey bricks,
We should tie-dye the walls, Make them really tick.
Cover them with murals, Go really wild
The perfect colour for every child.

Sofia, 12, Reading

∽∽∽∽

I think that girls should be able to wear pants in winter because their legs get very cold and they do not warm up quick enough.

Rebecca, 11, Warrington

∽∽∽∽

Is it fair that teachers get to wear their own clothes while we have to wear school uniform? No! Is it fair that teachers don't have to line up in the canteen? No! So let's sort it out. Teachers have too many rights.

Lauren, 13, Reading

∽∽∽∽

My dream school [is] a place where teachers wear uniform, we don't how cool!

Collete, 10, Coventry

∽∽∽∽

School, education centre, seat of learning, house of knowledge, academy. All synonyms for the place where the renowned English education 'takes place'. Despite themselves these do not bear much correlation to its true function. Conveyor belt or production line would be more accurate. Schooling is a process, taking in the many square, hexagonal and octagonal pegs and cutting off eccentricities to leave bare, uniform round pegs.

I do not pretend to have the answers only pose questions. But what I do know is that there need to be some serious changes. The journalists just state the news. The philosophers just state the facts about life. The politicians can change the news but don't. And apathy the great soother prevents people from changing their own lives. As Marx said, 'Philosophers only analyse life, the point is to change it.' Remember the girls and boys of today are the men and women of tomorrow.

Education … creates in the young people of today a cynicism and as Twain the great cynic put it: 'There is nothing sadder than a young pessimist.'

M . . . , lower secondary, Ilford

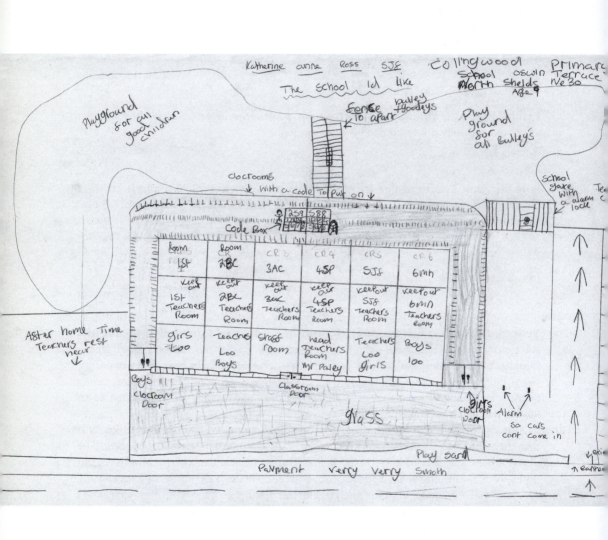

Katherine anne Ross   SJf   Collingwood   Primary
                              School   oswin Terrace
The School Id like   North shields   Ne30
                              Age 9

Playground   Fence buley floodeys   Play
For eul   10 apart   ground
good children   for
                                              all bulley's

Playground for eul good children

Clocrooms
With a code To Put on ↓

                                              School
                                              gate
                                              With a
                                              alarm
                                              lock

Code Box → 259 588
            470 940   A

Room CR1	Room CR2	CR3	CR4	CR5	CR6
1st	2BC	3AC	4SP	SJf	6mh
keep out 1st Teachers Room	keep out 2BC Teachers Room	keep out 3ac Teachers Room	keep out 4SP Teachers Room	Keep out SJf Teachers Room	keep out 6mh Teachers room
girs Loo	Teachers Loo Boys	Staff room	head Teachers Room Mr Paley	Teachers Loo girls	Boys 100

Aster home Time Teachers rest near

Boys Clocroom Door

Classroom Door

girls Clocroom Door

Alarm So cars cant come in

grass

Play sand

Pavment verry verry smooth

Chapter 8

Survival

'Schools may be getting good academic results but they are not helping the pupils as individuals'

Yet these blind fools will never know
What goes on inside this dreaded place –
Some cheat, some work, some sleep, some fret,
Some soar high, others low,
Just to emerge at last
As one of the human race.

R. (boy), 15, 1969

The need to create school settings that provide for children's well-being to flourish was recognised as early as the seventeenth century by Comenius (Forster, 2001). For exponents of early years and nursery education, such as Margaret McMillan at the beginning of the twentieth century, providing for children's physical and emotional health was a priority (Moriarty, 1998). Schools have, together with the development of welfare services, historically been regarded as one key element in promoting child health and survival. From the beginning of state education at the end of the nineteenth century, the home and the street were considered in many instances to be dangerous places for children and the school was regarded by many as a kind of 'life boat', saving children from potential degeneracy and immorality.

In recent years, pupils and teachers in the UK, the USA and elsewhere have been the victims of violent attacks perpetrated by outsiders or pupils themselves. This has drawn more attention to safety and security and has conveyed a sense of vulnerability. But schools have been places of violence from their beginnings. Stephen Humphries has drawn attention to the frequency of violent clashes, teacher with pupil, parent with teacher, pupil with pupil as well as children's organised resistance to the cane in his oral history of childhood (Humphries, 1981). Clive Harber has reminded us that schooling can be regarded as a violent institution and great harm can be perpetrated through the association of pain and fear with learning (Harber, 2002: 7, 11). In 1967, young people were moved to write about their hatred of corporal punishment which was not made an illegal practice in state schools in the UK until 1986 (Blishen, 1969: 153–63). However, in the accounts of children and young people's experiences in schools today, there is a strongly conveyed sense of vulnerability of self and others.

Since the 1970s, schools, through legislation, have had to become more aware of health and safety issues, and this has impacted on buildings and equipment. Doors and windows, walls and floors have necessarily been renovated to adhere to legislation. Over recent years, security cameras and monitoring devices, together with more stringent routines around access to schools, are apparent to children, parents and the community. School as a potential source of ill-health or stress-related illness is usually associated with teachers bowing under pressure and leaving the profession. But, for many children, school represents a difficult territory that they have to negotiate from the bus journey at the beginning of the day to the completion of homework at the end.

Many find their school to be a place where they do feel content, comfortable and cared for. School is for some children a place where they can find sanctuary from a frightening home environment. However, many write about the stress they experience arising from a number of school-based factors. There are environmental factors; the built environment is found to inhibit freedom of movement, dull the senses and allows no privacy. Furniture is poorly designed, is uncomfortable and its uniformity makes no allowance for difference in body size. Computers and their associated accessories take up large amounts of space in schools not built for them and children feel pushed out and cramped. These may appear to be insignificant grumbles but children are all too aware that a stimulating but comfortable environment is one which allows for better concentration. This was the case in 1967 when the participants of the first 'School That I'd Like' competition offered their thoughts.

> Wooden chairs! They're so uncomfortable! Couldn't we have some easy chairs, not deep armchairs but just comfortable backed chairs? The desks aren't much better; it's very painful to scrape one's knees on the bottom of them and worse still to knock one's hips against the edge.
>
> Ian, 16

School buildings were then found to be too hot in summer, too cold in winter, noisy and uncomfortable. Draughty, cold and unsheltered playgrounds into which children were dispatched without consultation was a gripe then as it is today. Describing his own idea of an ideal school, one youngster remarked:

> Three features of this school that would immediately strike a visitor comparing it with my present school would be: (a) comfort, (b) little noise, (c) efficient central heating and air conditioning ... conditions necessary for the most efficient, year-round learning.
>
> Ian, 16

There are many sources of stress which are directly to do with the physical environment and the material world of the school and these are referred to repeatedly in the 'School I'd Like' designs offered by children here. Many make a connection between a visually and pleasing environment and a sense of well being. This observation corresponds with studies that have shown a positive correlation between the degree of visual interest that pupils have and the frequency of disruptive behaviour in school settings (Wasson, 1980).

In reading these texts, what is strongly conveyed is a sense of vulnerability.

Children feel small; the school environment is hard, especially when you fall; space is limited; toilets are unwelcoming or inaccessible; sick bays are inadequate; buildings are noisy; corridors are hectic; the school bus is a daily ordeal; bullies threaten; teachers shout and seem not to listen; belongings can be lost or stolen; bags are heavy; lockers are damaged; minority students feel victimised and marginalised. There is enormous pressure to conform; to be different is dangerous.

Depression and associated suicide rates have been increasing in recent years among young males. Between 1970 and 1990 suicides among young men increased by 72 per cent and remained at a relatively high rate throughout the 1990s (McClure, 2001). Key findings from the Mental Health Foundation two-year study show that children and young people are less likely to suffer mental ill health given 'a high morale school offering a safe and disciplined environment alongside strong academic and non-academic opportunities' (Mental Health Foundation, 1999: summary of findings). It has been estimated that around 20 per cent of children and adolescents are experiencing psychological problems at any one time (Target and Fonagy, 1996). The UK-based charity, Learning Through Landscapes, recently conducted a survey in primary schools which revealed high levels of stress, with almost half the pupils experiencing some form of worry (http://www.ltl.org.uk/). A Child-Line study, Children and Racism (1996), revealed that 'many black and ethnic minority children in Britain endure blatant, unrelenting racist harassment and bullying on a daily basis' (Childline, 1996, in Grosvenor, 1999: 78).

Children desire that school be a 'safe haven', where they can be nurtured and grow into adulthood. Contrast this understandable desire which reflects their rights under the UN charter with the experience of many for whom school can feel like a torturous prison. Children's words convey with power their experience of school. It is vital that they be listened to and respected. When their experience is denied or ignored, the results can be tragic, as illustrated by the case of Vijay Singh of Stretford, Manchester. Vijay left these words for others to contemplate after he took his own life at the age of 13:

> I shall remember this for eternity and will never forget.
> Monday: My money was taken.
> Tuesday: Names called.
> Wednesday: My uniform torn.
> Thursday: My body pouring with blood.
> Friday: It's ended.
> Saturday: Freedom.
>
> (Grosvenor, 1999: 79)

There is, in the new millennium, a general expectation that schooling will continue beyond the age of 16 and the government is pressing for 50 per cent of young people to enter higher education by 2010. This contrasts with the late 1960s when most young people left school at 15 years and found work immediately. These contextual changes might account for the emphasis on 'survival' that emerges from the data collected in the 2001 competition, but far more influential are the pressures of examination which are today more frequent than anything endured by the youth of 1967, one of whom commented:

> Each year children are subjected to this violent treatment and then they are expected to develop into intelligent, well adjusted adults. School examinations as well as being cruel and ridiculous; a child's capacity for learning cannot be measured by such an immoral exercise. Examinations should be abolished, both internal and external.
>
> Loraine, 15

During the 1980s, Pollard, as part of his wider study of the social world of the primary school, noted that, 'the main source of stress for children in classrooms derives from teacher power and the evaluative context of schooling' (Pollard, 1985: 85). The latter has become far more pronounced in recent years as the number of exams or tests a child will experience has reached intolerable levels. Critical of the levels of standardised testing in the USA, Alfie Kohn has described the fact that children are tested to an extent that is unprecedented in our history as disastrous for learning (Kohn, 2000).

Compared with the past, there appears to be, in this collection of thoughts on 'The School I'd Like', a greater awareness among the participants of the need for schools to provide resources to counter the effects of too much stress in the lives of pupils and teachers. Unlike the 1967 youngsters, who rarely spoke of the need for a special facility in school to relieve stress, there are many examples given here arguing for rest rooms, meditation rooms and school counsellors to help support children in their lives. Stress is recognised as a condition of adult life and children appear to resent the fact that they might also experience harmful levels of stress.

In Europe, there are currently initiatives that are encouraging children to consider how their schooling contributes or otherwise to their well-being. 'Young Minds' is an innovative project aiming to explore, develop and demonstrate good practice in democratic (participatory and action-oriented) health education and health promotion in schools. Students from 12 European countries have been using ICT and cross-cultural collaboration in order to explore links between youth, culture and health (www.young-minds.net). Pupils from Iceland, Portugal, Macedonia, Slovenia and Switzerland have contributed their ideas about well-being and the school environment. There is a strong correlation between the contributions made by these children and those in the 'School I'd Like' archive in relation to identifying factors that matter in this respect. Almost identical features and aspects of school are noted as problematic. Small, cramped spaces to work or play within, lack of privacy, 'scary' school toilets, teachers' levels of competence and professionalism, the variety and quality of teaching methods, possibilities for student participation, examinations, criteria and type of assessments.

Young people from Macedonia (see Figure 8.1) set out the results of their brainstorming activities on well-being in school. They conclude:

> The larger problem in our school remains and that is the tension on the classes. Due to the style of communication that some of the professors have we feel very stressed out, uncomfortable, etc. It is caused by their bad mood, strictness in giving marks.
>
> (Young Minds, 2002)

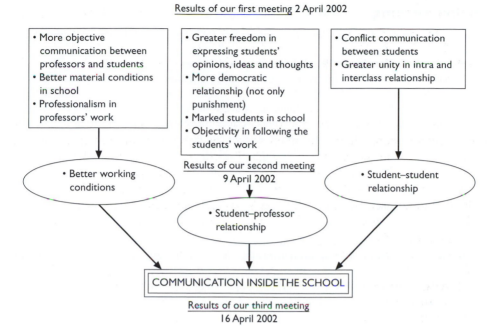

Figure 8.1 Macedonia school: about brainstorming.

Such a project shows the common experience of children in school environments and the advantages of allowing them to make connections between their physical and emotional feelings and their learning. A key finding from the project is the consensus that a healthier school is produced by increasing pupil autonomy and influence.

There are, in mainstream schools today, increasing numbers of children who are actively managing their health conditions. In the past, these children would have been removed from the mainstream and placed in special institutions. One of the striking differences that exist between the Blishen collection and the current collection is the increased recognition among children of the diverse needs of their peers. Not a single voice is raised against their integration within the school and an inclusive attitude is expressed in many of the competition entries. Included in the collection are the life stories of children who have struggled to fit in to a system, the organisational and design features of which are rooted in an era when the needs of the diverse community of children were not taken into account. Also included here are the ideas and viewpoints of children who are for short or long periods of their life accessing learning opportunities in the many educational hospital units that are organised regionally in the UK.

Further reading

Blamires, M. (ed.) (2000) *Enabling Technology for Inclusion*, London: Paul Chapman Publishers.

Blishen, E. (1969) *The School That I'd Like*, London: Penguin.

Connor, Michael J. (2001) 'Pupil stress and standard assessment tasks', *Emotional & Behavioural Difficulties*, 6, 2, May, 103–11.

Forster, J. (2001) 'Urban school buildings as educational environments: studies on the influence of architecture on children's learning'. Paper presented at the International Standing Conference on the History of Education, Birmingham, July.

Grosvenor, I. (1999) '"Race" and education', in Matheson, D. and Grosvenor, I. (eds) *An Introduction to the Study of Education*, London: David Fulton Publishers.

Harber, C. (2002) 'Schooling as violence: an exploratory overview', *Educational Review*, 54, 1, February, 7–16.

Humphries, S. (1981) *Hooligans or Rebels?: an Oral History of Working-class Childhood and Youth 1889–1939*, Oxford: Blackwell.

Kohn, A. (2000) 'Standardized testing and its victims', *Education Week*. Online: available at: http://www.edweek.org/ew/ew_printstory.cfm?slug=04kohn.h20 (accessed 16 October 2002).

Lightfoot, J., Wright, S. and Sloper, P. (1999) 'Supporting pupils in mainstream school with an illness or disability: young people's views', *Child: Care, Health and Development*, 25, 4, July, 267–84.

McClure, G.M.G. (2001) 'Suicide in children and adolescents in England and Wales 1970–1998', *The British Journal of Psychiatry*, 178, 469–74.

Mental Health Foundation (September 1999) *Bright Futures*, London: MHF.

Moriarty, V. (1998) '*I Learn to Succour the Helpless*', Nottingham: Educational Heretics Press.

Pollard, A. (1985) *The Social World of the Primary School*, Eastbourne: Holt, Rinehart and Winston.

Target, M. and Fonagy, P. (1996) *What Works for Whom: Implications and Limitations of the Research Literature*, New York, NY: Guildford Press.

Wasson, A. (1980) 'Stimulus-seeking, perceived school environment and school misbehaviour', *Adolescence*, XV, 59, 603–8.

Weare, K. (2000) *Promoting Mental, Emotional and Social Health: a Whole School Approach*, London: Routledge.

'Young Minds – exploring links between youth, culture and health', a web-based cross-cultural project coordinated by the Research Programme for Environmental and Health Education, the Danish University of Education. Online: available at: http://www.young-minds.net/ (accessed 16 October 2002).

Survival

My ideal secondary school is a safe haven, not a prison. It shouldn't be some-where you dread attending every morning, but somewhere you enjoy attending. I believe it should be social, as well as an educational experience. A school should always have a soul, there should never be a time when people are unhappy there, although there undoubtedly will be. At break there should always be laughter ringing though the corridors.

Angela, 15, Croydon

∽∽∽

The school that I would like would be a complete and utter racist and bul-lying free school! The teachers wouldn't be able to pick on the children that need help. There will be special classes for them to go to. The walls will have hidden cameras moulded into them so that there wouldn't be any stealing.

In place of the old, hard plastic chairs that you get, there will be huge, leather arm-chairs tailored for each pupil to feel comfy and warm. Tests should be relaxing and comfortable with Mozart or Bach playing in the background!

The rest room is a completely white room, with one sofa and table in the middle. On the table shall be a pair of top of the range virtual reality helmets, so if the pres-sure of school life gets to you, you can go in there with a friend and play for an hour.

Katie, 12, London

∽∽∽

I'm always tired at school because I have to get up early which makes it harder to concentrate on the work. So at my school, it would start later and finish earlier. I think that we get just far too much homework for one night (sometimes six subjects a night!). On occasions, I've started my homework as soon as I got in from school and didn't finish until ten! All that homework was getting so much that I was getting used to staying up late and when I did get an early night, I just couldn't sleep, I was so awake.

Alice, 12, Croydon

∽∽∽

The classrooms wouldn't be cramped and there would be fans in the corners of every room so in summer we wouldn't be so hot! There would be comfortable chairs that don't stick to your backside when you stand up, music playing (relaxing music to make us more in the mood to work hard, but not so relaxing we fall asleep!) and walls would be painted bright colours like orange and purple.

Hannah, 13, Ammanford

∽∽∽

The school I'm in at the moment isn't the school I'd like to go to. It has ugly blue, tatty walls, with massive dents and holes in the old walls. We have to share small desks, which you always clash elbows with your neighbour next to you. Some-times, if you're unlucky you will have the wrong teacher who is just so boring and strict that you are afraid to move, just in case he/she picks on you and gives you a glare, which could turn you to stone.

Scott, 14, Romford

∽∽∽

The students would like to have a better fire alarm system that could tell the hard of hearing (deaf) children because most schools have deaf children on the premises.

Chris, 12, Torquay

〰〰〰

School uniform is causing me torment ... The uniform that I wear for school is so horrible and uncomfortable. Like the huge heavy shoes that I have to wear through eight hours of school time ... Why can't I wear some friendly, pleasant, light trainers that are stylish and so much more comfortable than some boring, dull, depressing shoes? The blazers are the worst, they are like a hot blazing oven covering me and even in the winter I am piping hot.

Aaron, 13, Chelmsford

〰〰〰

There would be no homework at all. Home is for fun not catastrophes. Some pupils cannot get their homework done.

A.K., 10, Barnard Castle

〰〰〰

The tables would be higher & the table tops would be slanted so the pupils' necks don't get sore and it would be easier to write. The chairs would be higher as well and not wooden or broken. They would be slightly padded so they would be more comfortable to sit on. The corridors would be wider and would have lockers for all the pupils to use. I would have the stairs slightly wider so the people using them wouldn't get as squashed. I would have rooms that pupils could go to at the interval if they wanted.

Louise, 13, Glasgow

〰〰〰

If I could change my present school, the first thing I would do is get a decent bus driver happy and smiley that gives you respect, instead of being grumpy old men that never get a wash. The buses also have a horrid smell of cigarette smoke which makes me feel sick.

Laura and Sophie, 14 and 15, South Hunsley

〰〰〰

For Fitness and Health in my school there would be a swimming pool, an ice rink and a gym. On every desk there would be a lap top to do your work on and you can carry it about the school. We should have a bigger school so you are not crowded in the ground floor at the break and for safety going up and down the stairs.

Graham, lower secondary, Renfrew

〰〰〰

When exams were to be done, the pupils who take exams would have counselling regularly, so as to let them unwind. If a pupil is being bullied or is worried about something they'd have a counsellor on hand all the time, who would have experienced what the child was going through.

Megan, 13, Warminster

〰〰〰

I would like a room we could sit in instead of standing out in the cold freezing to death. ... I would like the seats in the school to be leather, the ones you can put your feet up on and relax instead of having a sore back all of the time. I also think they should make the tables nice and soft so that we don't have to lean on them and have sore elbows. If the school did what we asked, they wouldn't have to have a discipline system and we would also respect our school.

Samayo, 13, Glasgow

∽∾∽∾

Schools may be getting good academic results but they are not helping the pupils as individuals. Too much stress is placed on us, the pupils for exams and although exams are useful, teenagers can't cope with so much pressure.

In year seven when pupils first enter the school they do not really know what is going on and are usually quite worried about the first few weeks of secondary school. I think there should be volunteers from years nine and ten to 'adopt' a couple of year sevens. Then in their first year, if the year sevens had any problems or worries they could go and talk to these year nines and tens.

Joanna, 13, Wokingham

∽∾∽∾

Sometimes when the bell goes people get scared because you get pushed. I think the school should be more bigger and I think there should be a room – when you are bored you can go to this room and have a bit of a break.

Zhabana, 13, Glasgow

∽∾∽∾

I was six when I was diagnosed as clinically depressed and I'm fourteen now. I lost my mainstream school place because I was too bright for the class in which I was placed and yet no grammar school would take me in. Despite searching for a grammar school for me so that I could attend a school with a cohort at least twice my age, and despite paying for me at eight to study composition alongside undergrad-uates at the Royal Academy of Music in London, one day a week for a year, a place granted on the basis of my portfolio of scores, my LEA has only found one school willing to take me and *that* was a residential special school in another county. They didn't want me even to come home at weekends and they sought to shove me there despite my consultant writing that it would cause me serious emotional harm and my long-time occupational therapist that it would put me physically at risk. It did not rep-resent my ideal school but a nightmare that hasn't left me, of the naked power that adults exert over vulnerable children. The experiences one has as a child make the adult. Schooling damages and scars as well as nurtures.

Hero Joy, 14, home educated, Kent

∽∾∽∾

We think self defence is very important as you learn how to look after and defend yourself. If you are attacked you would be able to defend yourself ... it could save your life! That's why it's so important.

Ben, Lucy and Charlotte, 9–11, Daventry

∽∾∽∾

There would be a Quiet Zone (for reflection, meditation, rest) ... Reduce school bell volume. Have unsupervised study areas with comfy chairs and tables. Have water free and available ... Ban shouting. Get all teachers to understand a normal distribution applied to stress tolerance, happiness and creativity. From this knowledge, blanket or universal approaches of workload and timetable taught should be abandoned. And lastly, get teachers to practice empathy. This stays in the system and is the best preventer of bullying, something that every school that listens can imaginatively tackle.

Jonathan, 17, Manchester

∽∽∽∽

My dream school would have to have a few home comforts like a TV to watch while doing your homework, a drink and some food at your side throughout the day and maybe a C.D. player ... In fact, I think my dream would be my own home. I mean why go to school when you can have school come to you? I was thinking more along the lines of a special interactive computer so that you could do all your work online. But just because we're doing all our work on a computer and not going to that prison they call a school doesn't mean we don't get any playtimes. I mean it's unhealthy isn't it?

Paul, 11, Greenock

∽∽∽∽

Every child needs help, every child can give something special. For example, a child in care might need someone to chat to. Maybe she is very good in maths and understanding people who have problems with the way they are treated. To meet her need as well as celebrating her gift the school should set up co-counselling, that is where people doing the counselling actually get counselling themselves.

Kate, secondary, London

∽∽∽∽

I would like to change our sick bay.
It is a bit small, so I would like to make it bigger.

It smells of all the sick children who have been in it. I would like it to have a window, which could be opened to get some fresh air in. We have only got two chairs and sometimes children have to sit on the bed. I would like to have about ten soft chairs to sit on.

I would like to put the bed behind a curtain so that children can rest or change their clothes in private ... I would like to get some more sick bowls, which are smaller and easier to hold. I would like our new sick bay to be more colourful and to have fresh flowers for the teachers, helpers and children to enjoy.

Bethany, 7, Coventry

∽∽∽∽

We need lockers because of all those books I have to cart around. To make it worse I need another bag for P.E. which is like transporting a ton of bricks swung around my poor weak shoulder. If you think for a minute, this amount of luggage for one person would make you sweat; it does. Which makes me reek and pong, now that is not at all good as you can imagine. So my school smells like an unattractive place and stops people coming near me, especially girls.

Aaron, 13, Chelmsford

∽∽∽∽

Get each form or a group of students to re-decorate the classrooms with sensible colours that stimulate the brain cells – e.g. pale colours. The floors can be covered in special non-slip, easy clean tiles. We also need new quality windows and doors, not old damp and creaky ones. Also, if we had proper blinds then the students would be able to work in a decent light without having to move or get blinded.

Katrina, lower secondary, Romford

∽∾∽∾

In our school there is no uniform. We have marvellous toilets and showers. There are lifts for disabled people and ramps to slide down. There are still S.A.T.s but they are more fun and not as pressurising. Around the edge of the corridors are fish tanks. There is enough security on the school that there is no vandalism or stealing.

Carmen, 12, Sheffield

∽∾∽∾

I want my school to have a school garden with fountain and pond. There would be fish in the pond.

Christopher, 10, Surrey

∽∾∽∾

I would like a school with kind and quiet people and a teacher who would help me when ever I got stuck and at dinner time, when I walk into the dinner hall it would be quiet and not loud. And a school with friendly people in it. And I'd like a school where I would not get bullied in the playground and in school. And no bullies in the school and all the teachers are nice and friendly.

Jessica, 9, North Shields

∽∾∽∾

It would be good to have a nice 'spaced out' room where there is bright colours, noises, soft flooring and nice bright moving light.

Katie, 13, Middlesbrough (Hospital Educational Unit)

∽∾∽∾

I think we should have a quiet time for the last half hour in school. A quiet time would be where you just sat down and talked to the teacher about problems you were having at school.

Sarah, 11, Cardiff

∽∾∽∾

The School I'd like would have … a Health, Emotions and Problems building with trained counsellors and nurses to help you deal with your problems. There would be rest rooms for those who want to use it.

Jade, 13, Glasgow

∽∾∽∾

In my ideal school … the girls have a disco at night and the boys have football matches at night. There are beds for tired children and you can bring your pets into school.

Elizabeth, 6, Oxford

∽∾∽∾

We have a tiny concrete playground and a miniscule hall. The playground should be tarmaced for a softer fall.

Claire, 11, Cardiff

∽∽∽∽

'Sunnydales' is a school for young people who have been victims of bullying. This is a haven where 11–16 year olds from across the country can go to school feeling safe and secure because they know that the people they go to school with have been through the same traumas as them and so would not dream of bullying anyone else. The pupils would have normal lessons apart from one extra which would be CWB&SD: Coping With Bullying and Self Defence. A trained psychiatrist will always be available to help any students with any problems.

Jennifer, 14, Holbrook

∽∽∽∽

My ideal school would have normal lessons in a day but one lesson a week would be given up to relaxing and unwinding. This could be in the form of a sport, reading, playing games, singing or even painting and the purpose of it would be to relieve tension and enjoy unwinding. I think that this would calm down those students who are troubled because of the life they lead. I would also have a special musical room made for this idea where there would be lots of musical instruments to play and students could compose music.

Elizabeth, upper secondary, Suffolk

∽∽∽∽

I have a dream, that one day my school will be launched from paper and become reality. I have a dream, that one day children will be eager to come to school and will not be afraid of being beaten up or getting robbed.

I have this dream today!

C.L., 12, London

Part 4

Flexible contexts

Chapter 9

A sense of time

'I would like the school to be clever,
so it may last forever ...'

'What's the time?'
'Time you knew better.'

'What's the time?'
'About now by a good watch.'

'Time flies.'
'No it don't it goes on wheels.'
                    (Iona and Peter Opie, *The Lore and Language of Schoolchildren*, 1959)

Lemon and lime
Be on time.

(www.gameskidsplay.net/)

Time has long been a feature of the playground vocabulary of school children. Time though is a multi-faceted concept. It can be viewed as historical, scientific or mathematical. It can be imagined, experienced and measured. It can be theorised as geometrically rigid, with constant measurable distances or as percolated:

> Time does not always flow according to a line ... but rather, according to an extraordinarily complex mixture, as though it reflected stopping points, ruptures, deep wells, chimneys of thunderous acceleration, rendings, gaps – all sown at random, at least in a visible disorder.

(Serres, 1990: 59)

It hardly comes as a surprise therefore to discover that children and adults sometimes find time a difficult concept to understand and use (Hoodless, 1996: 8). Research in the first half of the twentieth century into children's understanding of time found that children, under the ages of 14 or 15 in particular, struggled to engage with the complexities of the concept. This research was profoundly influenced by the work of Jean Piaget, but since the 1970s a series of research studies have questioned the earlier findings of Piaget and others and have posed alternative analyses of the development of time concepts in children (Hoodless, 1996: 8–12). The evidence in the 'School I'd Like' archive supports the more optimistic view of children's capabilities in engaging with the complexities of time.

Time-consciousness pervades the texts. Many of the images of classrooms include a drawing of a clock mounted on the classroom wall: children visually engaging with time and pointing to one dimension of their school experience of temporality – the learning of 'clock' time. Children asked to think about the school of the future produced multiple narratives in the form of idealised morning, afternoon, day and week long timetables – an engagement with curriculum time. The timetables they produced are broken into communal notions of time as opposed to subject-defined divisions: 'breaks', 'play', 'dinner' and 'home time'. The asymmetry of time, in its distinctions between unequal categories of time – past, present, future – is made very concrete in children's reading of the past (their earlier experiences of schooling) their engagement with the present (critiques of the contemporary experience of schooling) and their speculations about the future (their understanding of how the present can determine the future).

Across Europe most pupils go to school for 150–200 days a year and the school day lasts between six and seven hours. In a year this attendance translates into somewhere between 900 and 1,400 hours (Stoll, Fink and Earl, 2003: 72). Children's understanding of time also translated into an awareness of how much time was spent in school: 'School is a place where you spend thirteen years of your life, from the age of 5–18'; 'We are at school for five days per week, 7 hours per day which leads us to having to concentrate for over 35 hours per week'; 'We see more of our teachers than our parents because it's five days a week about six hours a day'; and 'This essay has been written to show you what we as pupils think the school in which we spend 80% of our lives in should be like'. This awareness of the 'extensive' nature of school time, very much to the fore in the 2001 data, was often accompanied by critical observations and commentaries on current school organisation of the day and the week. Children were particularly critical of how school time invaded personal time: 'more time at home with our family and a lot more time getting to see the world and learn more things' and 'everyone needs a break – even the teachers ... Everyone needs time to see their friends and families so how are they supposed to get their endless work done?' There was evidence of a strong aversion amongst young people in 2001 to the regulated and segmented patterns of the school day, time organisation which was geared to the role of the school in producing adolescents who could easily make the spatial transition to adulthood, from one regularised space (school) to another (the workplace). Parallel to this aversion many children produced for the school of the future detailed and decorated school timetables which bore a close resemblance to current models of school time, both in terms of units of organisation and subject content. This evidence is suggestive of the effectiveness of schooling as a mechanism for shaping personal time, school as a training ground for maintaining the status quo in society at large. Such data are critical for understanding the child in the classroom (Austin, Dwyer and Freebody, 2003: 185).

Time in school was also seen as a precious commodity – not just for teachers. It was a scarce resource which children wanted to control. Children wanted their days better managed so that there was more social time – more time for eating and going to the toilet – and more learning time. Blishen's children and those of 2001 recognised that learning happens by design and is not a passive process. Some children advocated a progressive version of schooling – free expression, personal engagement with learning, and learner autonomy. The following voices are taken from Blishen:

> Step with me into a future school.

> We study at school for three days a week.
> For the last hour of the third day
> We hold discussions, in groups.
>
> Melanie, 14

⧓⧓⧓

> ... we believe that
> a freely-encouraged mind achieves more on its own
> than one pursued, hemmed in by a computerised timetable.
> School, for us, serves a purpose. We well know
> We are not here to pass exams (you look surprised!)
> But to learn to develop and respect ourselves
> By personal achievement.

> 'I hear, and I forget;
> I see, and I remember;
> I do, and I understand'.
>
> Elizabeth, 16

⧓⧓⧓

> In this type of school, free expression, free thought, freedom to work at one's own pace would exist. In this school, hours would pass pleasantly, 'lessons' would not exist because the pupils would have time to find out why, when and how.
>   *This* is a school! A place ... where people learn to reason, learn to understand and above all learn to think for themselves ... money is not what is needed so much as common sense, and the school I would like – in fact, the school I long for – would be a thing of the present.
>   *Now!*
>
> Judith, 13

⧓⧓⧓

> I hope that all the schools of tomorrow will primarily have much more freedom and variety than those of today. By freedom I mean much more time to work individually on subjects or aspects of subjects the pupils finds interesting; and by variety I mean more flexibility in the weekly programme of lessons.
>
> Gillian, 14

In the 2001 data, children demanded that the timetable give 'more time for the subject of your choice', that 'in a normal day, ... children would be able to choose one subject and keep at it for the rest of the day and that '[you] learn the subjects you want to learn for half of the week and the remaining lessons for the other half. This means that pupils can work better in lessons because they want to learn the subject'. Children may not use the language of the educational researcher, but they understand the difference between surface and deep learning, they recognise the importance of commitment, and are conscious of the relationship between motivation and learning.

In the few reported UK schools where a decision to be more flexible in timetabling has been taken, the results have been positive for pupil (and teacher) learning. Ingram (1992) engaged in a small-scale research project with seven year olds where they were able to negotiate their own timetable and curriculum. It was found that children worked at an appropriate level for their age, but did not choose the same balance of activities and subjects from week to week. More recently, the *Guardian* newspaper in the UK reported on the introduction of a flexible timetable at Leasowes Community College, a mixed ability comprehensive school in the West Midlands. The College since the early 1990s has designated Friday as a flexible day, when instead of the usual nine-lesson day, the children engage in a single activity – geography, art, basketball, and so on – over a five hour period from 8.30 am. At lunchtime the children are free to go home. The College's Director of Learning explained the rationale behind this creative use of school time:

> It allows teachers and children the time and space to work on projects. Many of the topics we are expected to cover in the national curriculum cannot be shoe-horned into a single lesson. What normally happens is that teachers have to … come back to it a day or so later, by which time they and the children have lost their focus.
>
> By giving children a proper time-frame to think about, develop and explore ideas and come up with some practical outcomes, they are far more engaged, and learn far more. Children like to see results, and they are sometimes hard to achieve in ordinary lessons.

The flexible day also had the effect of developing the important social skills of teamwork, responsibility, negotiation and listening; and pupil relationships with teachers and other adults improved. Not surprisingly pupils at the College were full of praise for its approach to learning: 'There's a friendlier atmosphere on Fridays and you've got time to think as things aren't so squashed.' The College is currently looking at ways of extending the flexibility so as to be more 'more responsive to the learner's needs' (Crace, 2002).

It was Charles Lamb who seems to be the originator of the adage that 'School days are the best days of your life', when he wrote in *The Old Familiar Faces* (1798): 'In my days of childhood, in my joyful school-days.' For Blishen's children, and those who responded to the 2001 competition, time at school held the possibility of being remembered as the most 'joyful' time in life:

> Once the fundamental difficulties are overcome, schooldays could well become the best days of one's life, the old sick myth becoming a reality and not merely a saying at which schoolchildren themselves instinctively cringe.
>
> Elizabeth, 16

∽∽∽

Once more back to the similar stark classrooms,
School times are the best times of your life?
Youth, school, do they mix?
It's beautiful to get older.
School is there
To be hated, loved,
To comfort, to hurt,
To help, to hinder.

Alizoun, 13

〰〰〰

I would like the school to be clever, so it may last forever . . .

Amy, 10, Bradford

〰〰〰

Thank you for taking time to read what I think school should be like in the future. As you now understand, I really think that school should be a fun place to be. After all, school days are said to be the best days of our lives!! I hope you have enjoyed reading my ideas about the future and that they help with your research. But who knows what school will be like in 100 years' time? All I know is that it is down to us and we can make a huge difference.

Anon., 11–13, Bristol

School years were and remain precious for children. In this context, and that of an era where schooling appears to be the in the throes of constant reform, it is useful to reflect on Larry Cuban's five clocks of school reform which operate on a different time zone:

Media time. This is the fastest reform clock of all, ticking every day and week.

Policymaker time. This clock chimes every two or four years as campaigns for national, state and local offices crank up to re-elect . . . incumbents or bring fresh faces to public posts.

Bureaucratic time. This clock records administrative action implementing what policymakers have decided . . . chimes when new rules are announced, revised budgets presented . . . [there is] a lag between policymaker time and bureaucratic time . . .

Practitioner time . . . moves at a much slower and uneven pace than on the other clocks.

Student-learning time . . . is the hardest to read because school-based learning often cannot be separated from home-based learning . . . [and there is] a lag time of learning over many years in a student's career in school . . .

(Cuban, 1995)

Cuban used this analysis to argue that the 'journey' from policy conception to changes in schooling is 'long'. However, his analysis of time also acts as a reminder of the multiple interests that shape a child's time at school. Further, other educational researchers have pointed to the volatile and very public nature of reform environments (Little, 2001). The interests of the child are generally heralded as being central to school reform, but school reformers and policy-makers should remember that a child's time at school cannot be repeated.

Further reading

Austin, H., Dwyer, B. and Freebody, P. (2003) *Schooling the Child. The Making of Students in Classrooms*, London: Routledge.

Crace, J. (2002) 'Believing in creation', *Education Guardian*, 17 September: Online: available at: http://education.guardian.co.uk/egweekly/story/0,5500,793086,00.html (accessed 19 September 2002).

Cuban, L. (1995) 'The myth of failed school reform', *Education Week*, 1 November. Online: available at: http://www.edweek.org/ew/ewstory.html (accessed 18 October 2002).

Hoodless, P. (1996) *Time and Timelines in the Primary School*, London: Historical Association.

Ingram, J. (1992) 'Starting from the child: a partnership approach to delivering the National Curriculum', *Early Childhood Development and Care*, 83, 121–32.

Little, J.W. (2001) 'Professional development in pursuit of school reform', in Lieberman, A. and Miller, L. (eds) *Teachers Caught in the Action: Professional Development That Matters*, New York, NY: Teachers College Press.

Opie, I. and P. (1959) *The Lore and Language of Schoolchildren* (1977 edition), St Albans: Paladin.

Serres, M. with Latour, B. (1990) *Conversations on Science, Culture and Time*, Ann Arbor, MI: University of Michigan Press.

Stoll, L., Fink, D. and Earl, L. (2003) *It's About Learning [and It's About Time]*, London: Routledge.

A sense of time

My perfect school, this requires a lot of thought! School is a place where you spend thirteen years of your life, from the age of 5–18, the time when you are most susceptible to outside influences are very impressionable ...

Edward, 15, Loughborough

∞∞∞

We are at school for five days per week, 7 hours per day which leads us to having to concentrate for over 35 hours per week, and this doesn't even include time taken to do homework each night. The pressure is always on.

I believe that at least once a week, preferably a Wednesday, each child should be allowed the choice of staying inside school or being able to do work at home using set tasks or projects. Another idea is that when each student gets this day off they don't have to do school work, they can exchange it for community service or work experience. This way each child would not have to concentrate for the full 35 hours that we have to do now ...

Katrina and Jennifer, 11–13, Romford

∞∞∞

School is in session at all times, twenty-four hours a day, seven days a week. It is the pupil's choice when to attend. They may break when they like, but be aware that other classes are taking place. They may wander at will around the extensive grounds and chat or play with their friends. The library is always open for a bit of extra study to whomever may wish to take advantage of it.

Anon., lower secondary

∞∞∞

It will have a new holiday set up; it will be open for about 48 weeks a year, but the children will have a set time to spend out of school. The children and teachers can choose when to have their holidays. This is very important because I think it's wrong for non-Christian children to get two weeks over Christmas and then have to go to school on Diwali or their own special days!

Kate, Secondary, London

∞∞∞

The day as a whole will be set at an easier time in the day to suit everybody. Instead of 9.00 am the day will start at 10.00 am. Thus giving the child the required amount of sleep to see he/she through the day. Starting later will mean two things, the child will be awake by 10.00 am and ready to work and also he/she will not be in a rush in the morning and will have time to be fully prepared. Living on the campus will also give more time to get there as we will not be constantly worrying about missing the bus or getting there on time.

Alexi, 13, Coventry

∞∞∞

A school day should begin at 9.30 am and finish at 2.30 pm. This leaves plenty of time for work and lots of time for play. A school week would last four days, Tuesday to Friday, and the weekend would then last from Saturday to Tuesday.

Stuart, 14, Bangor

∞∞∞

School starts at 9.00 am and ends at 3.00 pm, with two breaks during the school day, that is one fifteen minute break and another forty-five minute break. The first one is just to let the students have some fresh air and process what has been learnt so far. The second one lets the students have some lunch and take stock of the day's events; also chat with their friends.

Aisha, 14, London

∞∞∞

I think we should be able to come to school at 8 o'clock and finish at half past two ... so we can have more time at home with our family and a lot more time getting to see the world and learn more things. A bonus coming to school earlier would mean we wouldn't be just wasting our time at home doing nothing but watching the TV and sleeping and finally eating.

Jonathan, 10, Cardiff

∞∞∞

Well, I would start my day at 12.00 and end my day at 5.00. The first thing I would do was art class and then we would go to a nature reserve where we could hold the animals. After that I would go in the school's time machine where you could say hello to the Pharaohs and look at the mummies. But you could only stay for an hour. And then it was reading time and you would travel into the books. I like to stroke the horses in the books.

Felicity, 7, Oxford

∞∞∞

I would definitely get rid of assemblies because they just drag on and they are really, really boring. The long 5 day school week drags on too, we should definitely have every other Wednesday off to relax and do whatever, we could either study or just chill from reality for a day.

Anon., 11–13, Oxford

∞∞∞

Pupils of the twenty-first century should be encouraged to avoid worrying about school. At my ideal school as long as they have the twenty five hours of learning per week complete, teachers would not mind when they come, mornings or evenings or even weekends.

Stacey, 14, Stoke Golding

∞∞∞

. . . making school start a bit later than usual which is 8.45 and we would like to change it to 9.00 so that the children can have a bit more sleep.

Anisha and Ayesha, Primary, Bury

⧢⧢⧢

We want an extra break in the afternoon, as by that time we are tired out. We have one in the morning and at lunchtime but it isn't enough.

Alex, Jessica and Sarah, 12 and 13, Oakhampton

⧢⧢⧢

You may notice that the timetable has many more 'enjoyable' things included ['Adventure Activity', 'Choosing Session']. This is deliberate and with me being a child I know that I would work more enthusiastically if I knew that something 'good' was coming at the end of the lesson . . . Often I have found myself getting tired by the end of the day, and to prevent this we could have longer playtimes than you would normally find in a standard school. If, after careful tests, this is proven not to work the schedule could be changed, i.e. a 'rest' time at the end of the day where pupils sit and read for about half an hour.

Andrew, 10, Oxford

⧢⧢⧢

I think that we get just far too much homework for one night (sometimes six subjects a night). On occasions, I've even started my homework as soon as I got in from school and didn't finish until ten! All that homework was eventually getting so much that I was getting used to staying up late, and when I did get an early night, I just couldn't sleep, I was so awake! In my school, I would make sure that every pupil would get one or two subjects a night and none at the weekend because everyone needs a break – even the teachers – they'd have less marking to do! Everyone needs time to see their friends and families so how are they supposed to get their endless work done? I mean we see more of our teachers than our parents because it's five days a week about six hours a day. Isn't that enough work to be done without homework?

I am always tired at school because I have to get up early (seven o'clock a.m.) which makes it harder to concentrate on the work. It can get really tiring working until three o'clock, so at my school, it would start later and finish earlier. Not only would children like it, but so would the teachers! Out timetable has six lessons a day, and each lesson lasts for fifty minutes. School starts at twenty-five past eight so that means it finishes at three o'clock. I'd like to have four lessons a day, each lasting forty minutes. This would make my ideal school start at half past nine and finish at half past twelve, including the twenty minutes time of registration.

Alice, 12, Croydon

⧢⧢⧢

As for homework, I would prefer that students stayed on an extra hour and a half after school to be taught rather than going home and dreading the hours of work that lie ahead. Also this would mean that teachers would know the students' real abilities and not their parents!

Sarah, 13, Guildford

⧢⧢⧢

This essay has been written to show you what we as pupils think the school in which we spend 80% of our lives in should be like ... Homework! Don't you just love it? We as pupils do not, we have way too much homework which we find boring, a waste of time and no point. We would like to be able to use our creativity ... Our solution is that we write or draw or say what the lesson has been about in school at the end of the lesson so that you have more time to play when you get home.

I think that the key to success and learning is interest, support and, most importantly enjoyment. Spending an afternoon in a maths class with a middle aged woman groaning on about algebra really isn't my idea of fun! Talking to your parents about this proves a waste of time. Their response is that it's all part of school ...

We are supposed to get two pieces of homework per night spending 30–45 minutes on each, but it is guaranteed to take longer. Most homeworks require a lot of research and you do not always have the resources. Even though most households own a computer there are still many who do not and those children have a disadvantage. The main source of research seems to be the internet, and I myself do not have access to it. 'Use the library and school computers in your break time', I hear you cry. Our excuse is that we are given a break for a reason. Very much the same reason why working adults are given a break, our brains can only take a certain amount of information at any one time.

I think that the lessons are the right time duration (50 mins). The majority of the work is copying off the board, this is particularly boring ...

To most students break times are the most important time of day! They are a chance to chat to your mates, play football, and chill out.

Anon., 11–13, Bristol

〜〜〜

Now I shall move onto the onerous subject of homework. I have to admit that there is way too much of it. Some nights there may be at least two long homeworks to be in by the next day. You can spend from when you get home to about 8.00 at night, and that's only the first part! Homework should be given, but in small amounts.

The school day, I think should start later, for I'm not a morning person, and I don't think lots of other people are either. School should be from 9.00 to 15.00.

Melanie, 12, Ammanford

〜〜〜

In my ideal school you would learn the subjects you want to learn for half of the week and the remaining lessons for the other half. This means that pupils can work better in lessons because they want to learn the subject. We would have lots more breaks than we do at the moment! Four or five breaks between lessons should be enough (and that's instead of two). This would be better because then kids would be able to do the thing they love most – play! Plus, it has been proven that we do learn more in the playground than in classrooms so children might benefit from more playground time.

Rowan, 12, Hope Valley

〜〜〜

All the lessons for the pupils should be full and long with all the correct resources needed. The children need it to be a fun and average lesson.

Alex, 10, Cheshire

~~~~~

I think teachers should not be allowed to stop you while you are working on something you like doing every so often like computer work and should give you more time for the subject of your choice.

Tamsin, 11, Middlesbrough

~~~~~

I ... think it is an extremely good idea that every child should have a good education and have a bit more time to learn how to do it ... Therefore we need to have a longer time in school.

Bonnie, 10, Cardiff

~~~~~

In a normal day, the children would be able to choose one subject and keep at it for the rest of the day. At lunch time they would be able to read a book or use the internet. The teachers would also have the internet so that children could email them with their problems. In the end, the children would learn because they would want to learn.

Andrew, 13, Glasgow

~~~~~

I would change silent five minutes to more reading.

Ben, 11, London

~~~~~

Taking the register at the beginning of the lesson is a pointless time consuming activity. If each pupil had a swipe card then at the beginning of the lesson when pupils first go into the room they would swipe their card onto the computer next to the door. This computer would be part of a network ... The only downfall to this system is that a pupil could give another pupil their card and the other pupil could register them when they are playing truant. You would have to rely on the pupil's honesty.

Joanna, lower secondary, Wokingham

~~~~~

I think we should have a quiet time for the last half hour in school. A quiet time would be where you just sat down and talked to the teacher about problems you were having at school.

Sarah, 11, Cardiff

~~~~~

I think the time of the lessons is too short for e.g. in English when we watch a video on Macbeth the video is around 40 min. long which only leaves us with 5 min. to write what we think about the video. If it was that 10 min. longer we could write in more detail and could still have time to pack up and leave for the next lesson. And I think we should have 5 min. between each lesson so we can go to the toilets. And if we ask the teachers if we can use the toilets they say no you should have gone before the lesson.

Andrew, 8, Coventry

∿∿∿

I think we should have five minutes between each lesson so we can go to the toilets.

Ben, 12, London

∿∿∿

I go to lunch and realise that there is a mile long queue, I am not joking at all. So thirty minutes of waiting to get to the front of the dumb queue. All the edible food has chilled to the point of freezing and I have twenty seconds to eat my cold donut which was all that looked healthy at that moment in time.

Anon., 12, Chelmsford

∿∿∿

While waiting for lessons I think there should be chairs to sit on, magazines and a computer to play on.

Andrew, 11, Birmingham

∿∿∿

I feel the current system of academic progress is based too heavily on the birth date and not on the ability of each individual. For example, my younger sister was, in terms of behaviour, ready for reception when she was only two ... On the other hand, some of the children who were part of my class were clearly *not ready* and should have still been part of the informally structured, socially educating, Nursery.

I propose that each individual is sent to a kindergarten as soon as they are ready (this is decided by parents and regulated by the local education authority) and stays there until they are ready to progress.

The school timetable would operate in a staggered fashion, to avoid congestion and possible bullying by older larger students.

Robin, 17

∿∿∿

I would like the school to be clever, so it may last forever ...

Amy, 10, Bradford

∿∿∿

I dream of happiness and learning united. I dream of no interruptions. If I went to my ideal school I wouldn't wake up every morning and dread the next day, the next week, the next year, and the rest of my life.

Maisie, 14, London

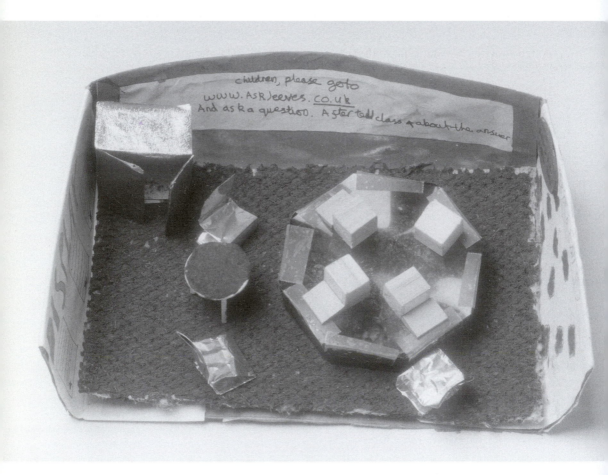

Chapter 10

Tools

'Pupils don't want state of the art blackboards or expensive televisions, they want comfortable chairs'

A concern with the material cultures of schooling has long interested English architects and designers. As early as 1874, E.R. Robson's illustrated *School Architecture* (1874) offered 'practical remarks on the planning, designing, building and furnishing of school-houses'. For Robson, the health and happiness of both the teacher and the child were dependent of the 'manner in which their school-houses' were 'constructed and furnished' (Robson, 1874: 7). Robson's colleague John Moss contributed a chapter on 'School Furniture and Apparatus', where he wrote:

> The furniture of the school-room should be graceful in form and good in quality and finish. Children are particularly susceptible of surrounding influences, and their daily familiarisation with beauty and form or colour in the simplest and most ordinary objects, cannot fail to assist in fostering the seeds of taste ... In our time it is desirable to extend the process of education ... by the adoption of good and tasteful designs as well as of superior workmanship for the necessary mechanical aids. The insensible influence thus exerted will not be without due fruit in future years, and, in the present, will assist in promoting a love for the school.
>
> (Moss, 1874: 360)

Similar sentiments were expressed in the 1930s when the Council for Art and Industry in England assembled an international committee of educationalists and design specialists (including the Bauhaus designers Walter Gropius and Laszlo Moholy-Nagy) to organise an exhibition in London for educational authorities and school teachers promoting 'design in education':

> it is important that the pens, the paper, the books, all the paraphernalia of teaching should be chosen with an eye and a touch for that which is stimulating ... that what is used in the elementary school may have quality of material, soundness of construction, fairness of colour and appropriateness of design, in sum beauty ... that educational authorities ... will buy with an appreciation of design and character even when it conflicts with a strict economy; that they will remember that they are educating the future consumer, and maybe setting a standard for industry in the next generation.
>
> (Council for Art and Industry, 1937: 1–2)

While such concerns are clearly critical in fostering aesthetics within formal learning environments they have more recently been identified as representing adult cultural values, a point central to the Vitra Design Museum 1997 touring exhibition 'kid size: the material world of childhood'. This exhibition explored and critically illuminated the changing relationship between adults and children as expressed in everyday material environments, including formal learning contexts. Classroom furniture and artefacts were shown to be potent carriers of meaning, communicating messages about adult notions and priorities with regard to the physical and psychological development of children. Furnishings and artefacts were invariably designed 'to fulfil the needs of adults, and even satisfy the fantasies, of adults' rather than addressing the notion of giving control to the child (Vitra Design Museum, 1997: 20).

So a welcome and unique feature of The School I'd Like archive is the wealth of material illuminating young people's views on design and technology. Many children used the opportunity of writing about the school of the future to identify current failings in the school environment. For example, Fiona and Rosie, respectively aged nine and ten, submitted a 'dossier' of captioned photographs and drawings identifying the material needs of their school in Durham:

> The blackboards are badly scratched and marked, the chalk doesn't rub off easily. The teachers need new chalk because they are always cracking pieces in half. We need new boards.
>
> The overhead projector in the infants is covered in sticky blobs so you can hardly see the screen. The school I'd like would have 2 brand new overhead projectors. There would be a lot more acetate paper [sic] as well.
>
> The heater is very rattly like a skeleton which is very annoying in assembly;
>
> 1   When someone wants to talk.
> 2   When someone is trying to listen.

Other children were critical of the design of music stands, paintbrushes and, particularly, chairs. The cry for 'comfy' chairs was accompanied by design solutions – egg shaped, dome shaped, chairs 'enclosing the head and waist', Swedish style, chairs 'with pockets and holders . . . [for] pencils, lunch, homework, diary etc.' One primary school year 5 group submitted designs for an 'electro chair', a vibrating chair, an automatic board and a pupil-friendly table. The 'Automatic Board' was a design development on the current whiteboard used in many schools. Either side of the board are mechanical arms – a 'writing arm' and a 'rubbing out arm'. Next to the writing arm is a container for holding different coloured marker pens. The 'enhanced' design features include:

Push the blue button and say what to write
Push the green button and say what to rub out
Pens easy for the arm to reach
Helps teachers to relax

The pupil-friendly table had twelve design features:

1 Button for extending and shortening legs plus digital size screen
2 Test scanner and digital result screen
3 Sticks of chocolate
4 Magnetic pad to retract pencil and teacher command pick up
5 Controller and PlayStation
6 Switch to turn screen from game to board
7 Slip to insert paper with game on
8a Penmaker
8b Pencil sharpener (electronic)
9 Magic book stand that takes you into story
10 Speaker to get you any story
11 Teleporter to take you home
12 Teacher instructions repeater.

The 'feel' of the classroom was also an issue. Floors should have carpets, brick walls should be covered, 'gentle music should be played' to help concentration and 'aromatherapy essences of grapefruit, lemon, orange and lime' should be sprinkled from above to stimulate and keep 'students awake in lessons'.

Computers feature regularly in pupils' descriptions of both contemporary and future classrooms. Research into pupils' experience of the National Curriculum in England found that pupils judged information technology as highly relevant to their current needs, were critical that enough curriculum time was not made available for it, and identified access to computers at home as a key success factor in their usage (Lord and Harland, 2000: 34, 42, 48, 50). Similar evidence was gathered by Crombie-White (2000) in his study of values and vision for the 'School of Tomorrow'.

The importance of the home as a site of IT learning has been a key element in the arguments made by the educational technologist Seymour Papert in analysing the impact of computer technologies in schools over recent years. He argues:

> As the number of these [home computers] reaches significant levels, we are beginning to observe changes in the relationship between teachers and students brought about not by a reform, but by the fact that the students have acquired a new kind of sophistication – not only about computers but also about ways to learn and methods of research.
>
> (Papert, 1997)

In a wider discussion about the staticity of school over time, Papert has questioned why it is that the introduction of computers into schools has not changed schooling significantly. Applying the concept of the 'grammar of schooling', Papert has shown how school culture works as a barrier to change. Innovation occurs in strict relation to past practice. Innovation is then so embedded in the old that the new is neutralised and loses its powerful function in signalling the possibilities of radical change (Tyack and Tobin, 1994; Tyack and Cuban, 1995).

Computers in classrooms, once new and strangely out of place, are now accepted as part of the 'grammar of school' and take on a limited role not defined by the possibilities inherent in the technology but defined by traditional pedagogy. Computers are used by teachers as mechanised instructors, performing a task normally carried out by the teacher: they are a 'teaching machine'. Students in 1969 viewed the computer in the classroom as a teacher substitute. For some this was a positive advance:

> I would use computers in my ideal school as I feel that this would cancel out any teachers' errors and this would mean that no child's education would be impeded by a teacher who is slow or inexperienced.
>
> Beverley, 14

Others were less optimistic and noted the limitations of computers as teaching machines:

> I feel there is nothing like a teacher's enthusiasm for his [sic] subject to make learning a pleasure, and I am sure a computer cannot show enthusiasm.
>
> Jeremy, 13

Thirty years later, many students still saw computers as mechanised teachers or robots, reflecting their experience of their use in schools. However, since children are accessing computers for play and socialisation from the home, they are bringing a new awareness of the potential use of computers to the schools. For example:

> Instead of having to hand write lots of notes during lessons, which is time consuming and boring for both pupils and teachers, information packs would be written on the computer to cover every subject in the curriculum as well as assignments. These packs would be accessible through the internet as well, so members of the school could view them at home as well as at school ... However, there is always the problem that the pupils won't actually remember all of the necessary information if they learn it in this way. If these data packs are compiled by both teachers and pupils, then they will be learning whilst designing the packs.
>
> Alice, 13, Bristol

Such a constructionist notion of the use of computers in learning stands in sharp contrast to the instructionist, curriculum led structure of schooling as it operates in the mainstream (Burke, 2001: 15). The 'constructionist use of the computer', as Papert points out:

> has no place in the grammar of school, which casts everything in the role of teaching device and thus, creates an assimilation blindness to the use of computers to support non-instructionist forms of learning.
>
> (1997)

It is obvious from this discussion that teachers and pupils share their classroom lives with objects. Artefacts are used all the time as a means of educating and controlling. Martin Lawn has argued for seeing the classroom as 'a social technology':

> It will be necessary to see the classroom as a hardware and a software; it is the material structure (spaces, walls, furniture, tools) and the working procedures,

series of ideas and knowledge systems, operating within it. The classroom is the integration of artefacts and rules and teachers.

(Lawn, 1999: 77–8)

Teachers bring tools together in simple systems for teaching and learning. An awareness of this process, of the classroom as a social technology, is evidenced in the School I'd Like archive. Children identified the connections between artefacts, the teacher and a system whereby learning can take place:

> We want new computers for our classroom. We would like a new scanner, printer and a new desk for the computer. Our teacher would like an interactive white board because it is easier to teach children with.
>
> J.H., primary, Belfast

∽∾∽∾

> I would put an interactive white board in nearly every classroom because then each teacher would only have to push the white board and the whole class would be able to see it.
>
> D. McC, primary, Belfast

This awareness of artefact, teacher and system was also evidenced in the many diagrams, paintings and three-dimensional models submitted. One model consisted of a classroom with rows of laptops, one for every child, encircling the teacher's electronic whiteboard.

Another feature of the visual material presented was the shared vision amongst children of what were the essential features of a classroom. Drawings and paintings of classrooms invariably contained the same features: pupils sitting on chairs next to desks, a clock on the wall, a teacher – usually female – standing at the front next to a blackboard [or whiteboard] on which is written the day and the date and either multiplication tables or short instructions, walls covered with letter and number friezes and displays, bookshelves, pencil pots, strip lighting on the ceiling, and a large cupboard. In short, classrooms were represented in ways that made them instantly recognisable through their signs and symbols.

The archive contains evidence of children recognising how teachers and artefacts combine into systems and extensive visual inventories of classroom signs and symbols, but there is a silence in this archive in terms of how children actually interact with the systems and objects. For example, the images produced by younger children include electronic surveillance, notably security cameras, doors with electronic codes, alarmed school gates and the 'brom-com' electric registration system. Children identify the 'watching' technology which is intended to both protect and monitor their activities, but as educational researchers we know very little about how children understand and respond to a system where the disciplinary and the pastoral are brought together through new communications technology (Peim, 2002: 6–7). Similarly, the blackboard/whiteboard features as an essential classroom symbol for children and they identify ways of improving its function, but our knowledge of interaction with this artefact is limited. A rare exception is a photographic essay by Peter Lyssiotis. The essay consists of a sequence of photographs taken of the same blackboard in the same room in the Humanities wing of a school. He chose to photograph the blackboard because for him, along with chalk, it was the most constant and recognisable badge of the education system. He found that the blackboard was positioned far above the eye level of seated students, so that the knowledge they received descended upon them from on high; from an authority who wrote on three tablet-like boards. It was a property which he found belonged to the teachers during lessons and to the students during break/lunchtime. For Lyssiotis the photographs reflected both his profession and the generation of students he was involved in schooling. They were also documents of his place of work. He displayed the photographs – repetition of one large general view, framing fragments of teacher instruction/explanation and student 'hit and run' comments – in a way which drew attention to the classroom as a political site, where dominant ideologies are argued for and reinforced, but also resisted through comment.

Classrooms and schools, teachers and pupils, work with and through objects all the time. Without special tools and routines (technologies), schools could not operate, yet this element of schooling is often ignored or obscured in research (Comber and Wall, 1999; Grosvenor and Lawn, 2002; Jewitt and Kress, 2002). The study of material culture, as applied to schools, involves a concern with the purpose of the technology, physically formed to produce a pedagogic or other effect; its processes of production and marketing; the meanings which surround their use – routines, scarcity, control; and the tensions and effects they produced. In this view, all objects, from rulers to ICT centres, are active, being social agents in themselves as they expand the range of human action and mediate meanings between teachers and pupils.

Classroom objects can act as memory triggers. A 65-year-old woman remembering her school days in Birmingham, England, in the 1940s and early 1950s, was shown a textbook and remembered:

> The only activities I was good at were dancing, gym and covering books. My own textbooks were covered with samples from a wallpaper book. We all had a textbook each to cover the various subjects. The headmistress raised money to help buy them holding Bridge evenings. I was very good at book covering, being neat and quick, and I would help out those less adept – this made me popular.
>
> (Marsh, 1998: 29–30)

'Classroom objects' have the potential to elicit indirect accounts of personal experience. Telling stories about objects can enable pupils and teachers to explain to an outsider the nature of school cultures, to make connections between events of yesterday and today, and to locate themselves in history. Stories about objects can provide us with fragmentary episodes of experience that can be added to material generated by more traditional methodological approaches in the construction of accounts of schooling. The data in the archive once again points to the importance of engaging with the viewpoints of young people. Their comments on objects and systems in the classroom help to reveal those very objects and systems and thereby remove their invisibility. Children, in their accounts of classroom life, to use Moss's comment of 1874, 'touch upon some points deserving of special consideration which might otherwise escape attention' (Moss, 1874: 402).

Further reading

Burke, C. (2001) ' "The School I'd Like": creating new archives of the history of education'. Unpublished paper from the symposium *The Subject in the Archive*, Network 17, History of Education, European Conference on Educational Research, Lille, 5–8 September.

Comber, C. and Wall, D. (1999) 'The classroom environment: a framework for learning', in Galton, M. *et al.* (eds) *Inside the Primary Classroom – 20 Years On*, London: Routledge.

Council for Art and Industry (1937) *Design in Education. Being an Exhibition of Material for Use in Elementary Schools, January 1937*, London.

Crombie-White, R. (2000) *The School of Tomorrow. Values and Vision*, Buckingham: Open University Press.

Grosvenor, I. and Lawn, M. (2002) 'Material cultures of schooling. Micro-histories of objects/routines'. Unpublished paper from the symposium *Material Cultures of Schooling*, Network 17, History of Education, European Conference on Educational Research, Lisbon, 11–14 September.

Jewitt, C. and Kress, G. (2002) 'Classroom visual displays as a sign of English'. Unpublished working paper, Institute of Education, London.

Lord, P. and Harland, J. (2000) *Pupils' Experiences and Perspectives of the National Curriculum: Research Review*, London: Qualifications and Curriculum Authority.

Lyssiotis, P. (1986) 'Look and learn', in Coventry, V. (ed.) *The Critical Distance. Work with Photography/Politics/Writing*, Sydney: Hale & Iremonger.

Marsh, A. (1998) 'The book coverer par excellence', in Morris, J. and Morton, P. (eds) *Through the Classroom Window*, Studley: Brewin Books.

Moss, J.F. (1874) 'School furniture and apparatus', in Robson, E.R. (1874) *School Architecture*, reprinted 1972, Leicester: Leicester University Press.

Papert, S. (1997) *Why School Reform is Impossible*. Online: available at: http://www.papert.com/articles/school_reform.html (accessed 6 October 2002).

Peim, N. (2002) 'New and old technologies of person management in the school – a brief history of productive governance in classroom social relations'. Unpublished paper from the symposium *Material Cultures of Schooling*, Network 17, History of Education, European Conference on Educational Research, Lisbon, 11–14 September.

Tyack, D. and Cuban, L. (1995) *Tinkering Toward Utopia. A Century of Public School Reform*, Cambridge, MA: Havard University Press.

Tyack, D. and Tobin, W. (1994) 'The "grammar" of schooling: why has it been so hard to change?', *American Educational Research Journal*, 32, 453–79.

Vitra Design Museum (1997) *kid size. The Material World of Childhood*, London: Vitra Design Museum.

Tools

We want new computers for our classroom. We would like a new scanner, printer and a new desk for the computer. Our teacher would like an interactive white board because it is easier to teach children with. Also on the computer we would like the internet because our school has a web site. It would be good to have a dust cover for the computer to keep the dust off the computer. CD-Roms are a quick way to get to other games. It would be good to get another mouse. It would be good to have a new overhead projector because our teacher has to use a G-clamp to help focus it to the screen. It would be good to have two joy pads to play games with instead of using the keyboard. It would be good to have speakers because if someone is working hard people can use them.

J.H., primary, Belfast

I want my school of the future to have a lot of computers, videos, telephones and televisions in the classroom, P.E. Hall and in the dining room I want a mobile so I can phone my parents if I am sick and also to talk to my friends and brother. I also want to have my own computer in my classroom, so that I don't have to wait for my turn and play the game I want.

I will also want to bring my videocassettes and watch the video's I want to watch. I still want to bring my books so you can read them. And I can write something I don't want to forget; I want to have my own desk and chair. I want to be able to e-mail my parents at work and my teachers, my friends in other schools, and my teacher can e-mail my homework to me at home.

Osa, 6, Orpington

The classrooms in my school would be decorated and furnished by the students themselves. Each student would have on loan a robust and easy laptop computer ... The desks would be set out so that you were not put in pairs but in larger groups where you could socialise with many different people and not be cut off from the rest of the class. The desks would have drawers in them that students owned and could keep their books in. The teachers would come to your classroom for most lessons. This would mean that students would not get backache from carrying their heavy bags around with them all day.

Sarah, 13, Guildford

The students are all given laptops at the beginning of their secondary education and they do not use paper and pen. Blackboards are only very rarely used so they are small and are easily rolled out of sight. The students also have desks that are easily moved so that the class can be rearranged i.e. in a circular pattern.

Aisha, 14, London

English isn't just a load of boring writing with sweaty hands and aching arms. In fact we don't really write at all. We just sit there talking to our new voice-activated pencils which at the slightest whisper jot down what you tell them to, as quick as lightening.

Jade, 9, London

〜〜〜

Don't feel that computer technology is going to solve your teacher problems. Although you may think the young generation are 'techno-whiz kids', desperate to try and experience as much technology as we can despite the loss of many valuable resources, most of us are *not* like that. We like using computers, but only as aids, and now even the use of the Internet has been dropping, indicating that people (although finding sometimes helpful and often extensive knowledge on the required topics) still want to use the 'tried and tested' methods of retrieving information. Remember that a good and varied education system is the basis for a truly successful country. Mistakes that you make now may well not be apparent for another twenty years when our economy starts to suffer from a narrowly educated workforce; lacking in imagination and the ability to think out things for themselves.

My ideal school would have a bigger boiler. My teacher would have a modern desk because he has a very, very old desk it is 70 years old and that was when our school was built. I would put an interactive white board in nearly every classroom because then each teacher would only have to push the white board and the whole class would be able to see it. Some people in the class may not have an computer at home and so the teacher could show them the Internet. My ideal school would have nicer curtains because the ones we have now are not very nice they are green. I would get the colour of the walls painted a different colour because the walls haven't been painted in quite a while now. I would fix the hole in the railings because some young children in the school got out of school and there is a river where they got out and it could be very dangerous.

D. McC, Primary, Belfast

〜〜〜

In each classroom each pupil has their own desk with a lap top. In the middle of the class there is a spinning board so you can turn it to each child. There is also a wide screen TV.

Group, Primary, Stedham

〜〜〜

All our classrooms should be big enough, in my classroom we are all squashed up because there are too many of us in a small space. Our desks should be high enough to get your legs under. The trays should not be built in under our desks, because you knock your legs on them and they rattle when we move and then you get told off for making a noise ... Chairs and desks that leave room for your knees ... All our classrooms should be bright, lots of windows and posters up on the walls.

Kimberley, 11, Alfreton

〜〜〜

In my dream school I would have top of the range computer systems, all linked up into one main 'teacher' computer. All work (except physical work, e.g. P.E.) would be sent to the teacher over the network. There would be digital books, pens and paper, saving trees, and the whole school would be environmentally friendly, as windmills and solar panels would power it. Each child will be able to listen to their own choice of music during the class, as most teaching will be done over a video link. Children will have their own laptops, so children who are ill in hospital or at home can still learn over the link.

Oliver, 13, Taunton[1]

∽∾∽∾

I would like an interactive computer wall in the classroom so we could link up with other schools. We could even have lessons from teachers around the world.

Jeremy, 6, Orpington

∽∾∽∾

We should have electronic white boards to help the teachers and get lessons over quicker.

Hannah, 10, Richmond upon Thames

∽∾∽∾

What us students can never understand is why the teachers get better chairs than us, even when they just sit there and don't do much! I can agree that they may be older and more fragile, but so are we! Well, we are young but we are developing so we need comfortable chairs just as much.

Jennifer, 12, Romford

∽∾∽∾

In classes the students sit in egg shaped chairs, the student leans back and in the top of the chair is a sprinkler, which sprinkles aromatherapy essences of grapefruit, lemon, orange and lime. These essences are stimulating and are designed to keep them awake whilst in lessons.

Harriet, 17, Shrewsbury

∽∾∽∾

There would be soft bean bags to sit on and there would be a lovely soft carpet on the floor.

Greta, 8, Leeds

∽∾∽∾

1 Written while an inpatient at the Children's Education Unit, The Children's Unit, Musgrove Park Hospital, Somerset.

The classroom, where it all happens ... with hard plastic chairs. We have to work on them 5 days a week, and I can tell you, it isn't the most wonderful experience ... The uncomfortable bit is the desks and chairs. The chairs could be a nice shape and have padding.

Melanie, 12, Ammanford

❦

The tables are another matter. At the end of the year, your knees are hurting so much you are sure that they have done some permanent damage to the top of your legs. There are pencil marks on it and ruler scrapings on the edges.

Natalie, primary, London

❦

I would like lockers to put all our books and PE kit in. I think the windows should be cleaned at least once a month. The blinds should be white instead of black. We should have soft chairs and nice tables and we should have nice soft carpets. There should be water coolers all around the school.

Lisa, lower secondary, Glasgow

❦

I would like the seats in the school to be leather, the ones you can put your feet up on and relax instead of having a sore back all of the time. I also think they should make the tables nice and soft so that we don't have to lean on them and have sore elbows.

Samayo, lower secondary, Glasgow

❦

We choose circular tables with computers so that every child can see and feel that they are working in a fun atmosphere to make them feel more relaxed. The circular tables enable each child to see each other and feel part of a group. Dome chairs will induce comfort and a responsible environment in which the pupil will work. The enclosed speakers will give full surround sound without the sound interacting with other students. The chairs will have pockets and holders to hold pencils, lunch, homework, diary etc ... The chair will be in a 70's dome style enclosing the head and waist.

Dominic and Benjamin, 11 and 12, Colchester

❦

I would have comfortable chairs to make the lesson more interesting; chairs like the ones in offices would support our back and mean we would not fidget, and would therefore pay more attention to the teacher.

Matthew, 17, Reading

❦

We don't have much equipment but we do have some. We should have chairs with cushions for assembly your bottom gets sore and its not very comfy to sit on the floor.

Rebecca, 11, Cardiff

⬿⬿⬿

In geography it would be great if we could have tables with maps on them covered with glass or plastic so you could use them if you needed for quick reference.

Rachel, 13, Reading

⬿⬿⬿

In art you will use electronic circuits under a metal board to make a picture with flashing lights.

Gautier, 8, London

⬿⬿⬿

We wouldn't have a board (black or white) because all they are used for is to project/write things for kids to copy. There would be absolutely NO COPYING in my ideal school because it doesn't teach you anything.

Rowan, 12, Hope Valley

⬿⬿⬿

Our classrooms are disgraceful. If you don't believe us come and have a look.

Matthew and Rhys, 10, Cardiff

⬿⬿⬿

A school which would want to educate pupils fully and comprehensively would need all the correct equipment and resources. If the school wanted students, the school would have to attract the parents by the facilities, size and its appearance. A school should make its pupil welcome and comfortable. There should be perfect carpet on the floor and wall paper, not showing the red naked brick wall itself. The classrooms should have neat tables and chairs, one large one for the teacher, it should have several display desks, a couple of glass windows, two or three computers and two different sex toilets for boys and girls instead of disturbing students by running down the corridor and make echoing noises.

Alex, 10, Cheshire

⬿⬿⬿

Our music stands are hopeless. Most of them are broken, you can't put your music on them without it swinging 'round or falling over. It's not good enough. We should have decent music stands to play music because we just can't manage it.

Catherine and Rosemary, 9 and 10, Durham

⬿⬿⬿

In art we need better paintbrushes. The ones we have at the moment are quite fat and it is impossible to do work with fine lines, to do this we need thin brushes.

Delyth, 10, Cardiff

My Perfect School

Disabled access around the school

Swimming pools for lessons

School holidays and trips

Seperate halls for gym, food and assembly

Smaller classes

Shallow

Food

assembly

my new class

gym

experience

Class pets.

modern uniform

Adventure play ground

lap tops to work on.

after school club for parents who work late.

after school club

Final words
Whole school visions

School, A.D. 2000
A computer lies obsolete in the corner,
Good only for last year's curriculum:
But now a robot master plugs itself in
To obtain facts which it must pass on.
A siren warns the form that class begins.
The boys lie in anthropomorphic chairs,
Ease on their earphones and listen to
The toneless voice of the robot.
Briefed from the master robot he poses a question:
'The constituents of a cathode compound?'
Electrically operated plastic arms
Elevate above the polyether chairs
To signify they know the answer,
And boys mumble answers into their crystal mikes.

C. (boy), 13, 1969

Imagining the possibilities of education is inevitably shaped by the realities of the present and the mythologies of the past. Fundamental structures of schooling are seemingly impossible to shift at anything more than an experimental level. Progressive ideologies of education have existed since the idea of state education was first envisaged, epitomised by William Godwin's warning of the invidious intentions of the establishment in perpetuating, through mass schooling, its position of authority (Godwin, 1793). Near the end of his life, the philosopher and educationalist, John Dewey, remarked on the seemingly impermeable and resistant nature of the institutions of schooling in spite of logical and research based arguments for reform. He noted how changes that did occur were merely 'atmospheric' and had not 'really penetrated and permeated the foundations of the institution'. The 'fundamental authoritarianism' of schooling survived unscathed (Dewey, 1952: 129–30, in Kohn, 2000: 7).

To open up a debate among and between children, teachers, parents and the wider community about the process and products of learning in the twenty-first century is an act which recognises that key assumptions about the nature of childhood and the rights and responsibilities of individuals have altered significantly in recent decades. Arguably, the institutions conceived of as beneficial to children and society in the past, based on the idea of the child as dependent, without agency and lacking personal autonomy or individual rights, come under increased strain as they conflict with contemporary conjectures about children's place in society. The sociologist, Anthony Giddens, has discussed the crisis in the notion of the family in the wider context of what he has called 'a democracy of the emotions' (Giddens, 1999). Similarly, mass schooling, as an institution which was born in an age when children were 'seen but not heard', rooted in the acceptance of a fundamental imbalance of power, is today in crisis as it struggles to continue to be shaped around past assumptions about the relations between adults and children. Both the institutions of the family and the school have risen to the top of the political agendas of all political parties in the UK and elsewhere as they fight for the moral high ground, usually with a call for a return to 'traditional' values or practices. Traditionalists have responded by calling for a return to past 'certainties' (Woodhead, 2002).

The year 1967, when Blishen's young voices were collected, was significant in the history of education in Britain. The Plowden report, *Children and their Primary Schools*, was published, placing the child at the heart of education. The report advocated the use of discovery learning, first-hand experience, environmental awareness, interdisciplinary approaches, and group work as ways of capturing pupils' imagination (Plowden, 1967). The Campaign for Comprehensive Education was launched amidst a climate of reform brought about by the return of a Labour government. A report by the Comprehensive Schools Committee was to recommend that all direct grant schools be integrated into the comprehensive system. It was a time of immense educational change and optimism (Birkett, 2001). In contrast, after a period of legislative reform in schools following the 1988 Education Reform Act, the early months of 2001 saw recognition of a growing crisis in the UK teaching profession as many experienced teachers were opting out through early retirement and severe gaps in provision were reported. There were 44 per cent vacancies in London, 26 per cent vacancies in south east England and a shortage of subject specialists in maths, science, design and technology (BBC News, 21 September 2000). Some teachers were opting out before they even began. Teacher trainees in HE institutions were reportedly beginning to seek their future employment outside of the school sector and inside the new leisure or culture industries (Peacock, 2002). Schools were reported to be on the point of 'melt down' with severe and growing demoralisation within the teaching profession. The journalist Nick Davies had recently published a series of scathing reports on the condition of state schools in Britain concluding that: 'The evidence that poverty undermines education is overwhelming – and has been for decades. Yet governments deny it. The last government denies the poverty itself. This government admits the poverty, but denies its impact' (Davies, 2000: 8). Indeed, it could be said that the emphasis on raising standards and promoting higher achieving schools in order to return results in the short term had perpetuated the neglect of tackling fundamental and pervasive problems within the school system as a whole. This short-sightedness has also helped to shape research interventions in schools where opportunities are more likely to be associated with short-term efforts to evaluate and improve specific educational programmes than with long-term efforts to understand entire educational systems.

In 1999, the UK Qualifications and Curriculum Authority (QCA) commissioned the National Foundation for Educational Research (NFER) to conduct a review of research on student experiences and perspectives of the national curriculum. This was completed in March 2000, and updated in the spring of 2001, just at the time when children were invited to offer their views on 'The School I'd Like'. A review of this literature reveals:

- the majority of research fields are small, i.e. comprising less than 100 pupils.
- research methodology is predominantly qualitative, the group interview being particularly favourable and questionnaires are used in many cases.
- subject-specific research, with particular subjects featuring repeatedly, is predominant and there is a dearth of research which looks at cross-curricular or progressional issues.
- recently, there has been a rise in the number of research projects which focus on assessment and levels of achievement.
- secondary education is more subject to research than primary.

A major ongoing research project in this area is the Economic and Social Research Council (ESRC) supported Network Project, *Consulting Pupils about Teaching and Learning*, which focuses on 'ways of increasing motivation, commitment and attainment through the effective use of pupils' perspectives on teaching and learning'. The Network aims to support teachers in primary, middle and secondary schools in developing 'manageable strategies for consulting pupils about their experiences of learning and in evaluating the outcomes of these approaches' (Ruddock, 2002). Engaging pupils more in teaching, learning and 'achievement' are the principle concerns of this research agenda. An important part of its purpose is to publicise good practice in incorporating pupil voice. However, 'School' and 'Schooling' is not in question; the objective is not to question the foundations of school itself. The fundamental structures and characteristics of school are taken as given.

This is typical of school-based research where school environments and classroom environments have tended to be researched or studied as separate spheres. It has been suggested, 'School effectiveness researchers do not always study classrooms closely and classroom research has not often studied school level effects' (Pelligrini and Blatchford, 2000: 90–1). Jerome Bruner (1996) has noted how the focuses of research around standards, performance and achievement have led to a neglect of the intimate nature of teaching and school learning.

So what is the contribution of the School I'd Like archive to current discourses on teaching and learning and the future of school? It is, of course, possible to bring to the archive questions of current concern in education such as the pupil perspective on testing, homework, specific subjects, bullying, the national curriculum, buildings and facilities, the use of I&CT in learning. But there is much in the archive which transcends such compartmentalisation and considers critically the very reason for school, the meaning of its structures and hierarchies, the purpose of 'schooling'. These questions are seldom asked by researchers in the field because they do not lend themselves to short-term practical solutions towards school reform or improvement.

Here, children and young people have provided evidence of how all aspects of school and schooling interrelate from their perspective and, indeed, how the school and its immediate landscape connect with the community. They reveal, in their passionate responses in words and images, a dynamic which is missing from much exploration into the nature of schooling. How school feels, smells, tastes, its rhythms and rituals, its meaning and significance are revealed all at once in writing, drawing, modelling and planning, which attempt to capture whole school visions.

In making sense of the vast quantity and variety of responses, like Blishen before us, we have drawn up themes which seemed to arise from the data and connect with current debates and discourses about education for young people. However, like Blishen, in selecting from whole entries extracts which spoke to those themes, we have not been able to show how the various parts of school form the whole as experienced and envisaged by children and young people.

Therefore, we will close with some examples of how children and young people have addressed the question of school as a whole, not only showing recognition of how the different parts of schooling interconnected but also to envisage how this interconnectedness might be redesigned. In their words and images describing school as they experience it, they reveal their priorities for change. In sum, they do not want something that was designed for a different time. However, while they have their visions, the history of education tells a story of institutional change on the surface, but fundamentally the classroom, its routines, the regimentation of life, the lived experience of school does not change, a fact recognised periodically through-out time by commentators and, sadly, by some children who wrote about the future but expected adults to fail them yet again.

Further reading

BBC News, Thursday, 21 September, 2000, 16:24 GMT, 17:24 UK. Online: available at: http://news.bbc.co.uk/1/hi/education/935984.stm (accessed October 2002).

Birkitt, D. (2001) 'The school I'd like', the *Guardian, Education Supplement*, 16 January 2.

Bruner, J.S. (1996) *The Culture of Education*, Cambridge, MA: Harvard University Press.

Crombie-White, R. (2000) *The School of Tomorrow. Values and Vision*, Buckingham, Philadelphia: Open University Press.

Davies, N. (2000) *The School Report. Why Britain's Schools are Failing*, London: Vintage.

Giddens, A. (1999) 'Runaway world', The BBC Reith Lectures, Lecture 4, December 1999. Online: available at: http://www.lse.ac.uk/Giddens/pdf/1-Dec-99.pdf (accessed October 2002).

Godwin, W. (1793) *Enquiry Concerning Political Justice*, 1971 edn., Codell Carter, K. (ed.), London: Oxford University Press.

Kohn, A. (2000) *The Schools Our Children Deserve. Moving Beyond Traditional Classrooms and 'Tougher Standards'*. New York, NY: Houghton Muffin.

Peacock, A. (2002) 'Making the environmental message more effective: working with children for ecological awareness at the Eden Project'. Paper presented at the 'Beyond Anthropocentrism' conference, University of Exeter, 16–17 July.

Pellegrini, A. and Blatchford, P. (2000) *The Child at School: Interactions with Peers and Teachers*, London: Edward Arnold.

Plowden Report (1967) *Children and Their Primary Schools*, London: HMSO.

Rudduck, J. (2002) 'Consulting pupils about teaching and learning', ESRC Network Project. Online: available at: http://www.consultingpupils.co.uk (accessed October 2002).

Woodhead, C. (2002) *Class War. The State of British Education*, London: Little Brown.

Final words

There is no school in the world that I would like because they are all the same. You come in very early, very tired and you have to walk upstairs all day and sit at a desk day after day, but that is not what I want. I want to get excited when I go to school, I want to go and know there is a chance. I would want the school to be a bit bigger so that is lots more room to walk about in the corridors ... There is one thing I would change but I don't know if many people would agree with me about. Making school voluntary, let the children decide because overall it is their life if they don't want to have qualifications fine it is their life and it saves teachers from wasting their time because they would be teaching pupils which aren't going to use anything they have learned, and don't care about what happens to them in the future.

Ryan, secondary, Renfrew

〰〰〰

The perfect school; is there such a thing? Is it possible to engineer a place where students and teachers can work in harmony, where people respect and care for one another, and can manage to make education interesting and fun? To be frank I think it is verging on the impossible, however if I was to design a school which I would gladly get up at 6.30 am every morning to get ready for, it would have to be a bit abnormal!

Susan, 16, Llangollen

〰〰〰

The school I'd like would be situated in my own bedroom. Here, there would be a telephone, a computer (or a laptop) and a television where you could interact with your teacher. This idea is on the cutting edge of technology and is based on the children in Australia, who live out in the 'bush'.

You would get your work from each of your subject teachers either weekly or monthly by email. For lessons such as Design Technology and the Sciences, you would book a place by computer or telephone for the course you wanted to take. Then you would go to the local education research centre (a local laboratory) at the time of your course and there would be a teacher and other children present for the practical lesson. You could stay there as long as you wanted, and do as many courses as you had booked yourself in for. However, each week you would have to go on at least two courses to improve your Science and Design Technology skills and to give you a break from just staying in your house. The lab caters for four subjects which are Physics, Chemistry, Biology and Design Technology. You would not need to take any equipment with you because the lab would provide it. Yearly, you would have a small fee (i.e. thirty pounds) to pay for the privilege of using the laboratory. The reason for using the laboratory is so you can do the experiments for your subjects, instead of just doing written work. Also you can do the experiments safely and meet other people.

Other lessons such as Maths and English you would do from the comfort of your own bedroom. You would receive your work through the computer by email. If you got stuck you could phone your subject teacher up or send them an email or interact with them through your television. You would also receive an email saying when you would be able to turn the television on and interact with your teacher.

When it comes to exams, at the moment the teachers try to help you but their advice can be contradictory. I hope in my 'Bedroom School' the revision guide would be easier to understand and the information would be the same from every teacher. As well, the teachers would provide a way for the revision to be fun and fit in with your social life. The exams will happen in the Lab where there will be teachers supervising you. You would be able to use your computer in the exam if you wanted to. However, you would not be able to ask for help.

When it comes to being able to express yourself at the moment in ordinary schools you are very confined. Your free time is limited and you can't choose some activities because you would look uncool. Other times you don't want to join an activity because people you don't want to be with have joined up. With my virtual school you would be able to follow instructions for some activities at your own house. As an example, you would be able to turn your television on at a certain time and a teacher would be giving instructions on how to cook. When it comes to sports, you would book courses at your local leisure centre at least twice a week to do activities of your own choice i.e. swimming, netball, football, karate, gymnastics, ballet, rugby, hockey and athletics. This enables you to keep fit and gives you the freedom to choose the sports you feel comfortable with.

With the 'Bedroom School' some great advantages are that you don't need to pay excessive transport costs. As regards transport to the Leisure Centre and the Lab you could buy a monthly bus ticket, which is still cheaper than paying school bus fares or going by car. It also means you save travelling time so you can get your work done quicker so you can have more leisure time.

Another huge advantage is you would be able to work quietly without being disturbed. In classes at the moment people are silly and noisy and are trying to see how far they can go before the teacher gets angry. This results in the teacher getting cross and five minutes of the lesson goes up in flames. With my school you can work without disturbance, at your own pace and if you get stuck you could interact with your teacher or phone or email them.

Louise, 13, Uttoxeter

≈≈≈

The school of the future
While we are having literacy hour it is so cramped in class.
Rooms need to be bigger or less people in each class.
We should use the computers more as whatever job you want to do you have to know how to use computers.
Shutters should be put on all windows so that they cannot be smashed.
We should have more Art because too much time is spent reading and writing.
Canteen chairs are nice but some are too small for the junior children.
We should have a swimming pool in school so that we don't have to go on the bus. We would be able to have more swimming lessons.
More school trips to places of interest because when you can see what we are learning about it is easier to remember it.

Ian, 9, Liverpool

≈≈≈

I would have a mini zoo so that the younger section of the school would learn some more about animals. Every pupil would have a rota to choose what they would do that day. If there were people who were naughty the teachers would choose for them the next day. At play time the supervisors would hand out snacks for the people who didn't bring a snack. In the playground there would be a net ball stadium and a footy pitch. In the staff room the teachers would have a big coffee table and some shelves to store things. Inside the building there would be a skating rink for those who want to skate and learn. There would be a special room to hire your skates but if you wanted to you could bring your own. If you were feeling ill you could go to a special room with bean bags and books while you were waiting for your Mum or Dad to pick you up from the school. The school would keep animals like pigs so that children who wanted to be a farmer in the future could learn how to look after them.

Georgina, 8, Norwich

～～～

I want mufty not uniforms
I want packed lunch not school lunches
I want boys and girls not one sex
I want three subjects a day not six
I want to be taught by robots not teachers
I want more sports than lessons not the other way round
I want classes based on ability not age
I want sport teams for every pupil not just for the ones that are good at sport
I want in history to go back in time not just learning from T.V. and books
I want cakes and sweets every day not just on people's birthdays
I want breaks indoor OR out not just out
I want lockers that lock not pull lockers that you open
I want every classroom to have air conditioning and heating not one of the two
I want to have tame dogs and cats running around the school not just plants
I want to have 5–10 computers, 5–10 T.V.s and 5–10 phones (that pupils can use in every classroom not just one each)
I want lessons on the moon, the beach, and the school roof not just classrooms
This is the school I'd like to have.

Emma, 8, London

～～～

Schools today are very boring, so I've got a list of changes to be made.
I think the classes should be changed so that there is more fun and things to do. The classes should be interactive so you learn and do things.

The school should be in a different location maybe in a big field so there is lots of room to play. Smaller brighter and lots of displays inside, more computers in each class and longer break.

The lessons should be more fun and special teachers. Less maths and more P.E. and less language and more drama.

The teachers should be nicer, no shouting or screaming and be lenient unlike they are today.

School should be an hour shorter and more half days.

There should be more fun trips like to the cinema and swimming you should have a different school comp every year.

So generally more fun and play than there is today.

Craig, 10, Edinburgh

〜〜〜

To achieve better age-integration in society, I would like to see a weakening of the association of schools with children. Ideally, although I have some reservations as to the economical practicability, I would like to see an optional and comprehensive education system for all ages. This would help relationships between people of different generations, and give greater freedom to the young. Education should be free and accessible for everyone, as the right to information and understanding of the world is fundamental, and independent of financial status. The system should be flexible enough to allow people to specialise and follow their own interests and talents, and to catch up on other areas later on, if necessary.

The school I'd like would stand for freedom, tolerance and flexibility. The school would be run by the whole learning community. Members of the community would support and respect each other, and nobody would be victimised or humiliated. There would be an atmosphere of cohesion and unity, avoiding segregation where possible. Students would be able to learn at their own pace, the school acknowledging their differing circumstances. All people would be valued, and enabled to develop their own abilities to the full, whether these be practical, academic, social, physical or artistic. It would be a place where students of all ages came voluntarily, because they actually wanted to be there.

Lorna, 14, Ipswich

〜〜〜

The perfect school would have to really focus on the social side of life, as that is really the best part of everyday school. Not the academic part of school, but meeting new people and making both friends and enemies. However in the perfect school I think you should still have to do lessons as that is the current reason for going to school in modern life and it is very important as it prepares you and gives you important skills for later on in life. However children and, especially, teenagers get so fed up with the current way of education that they actually do not learn as well as they could do as they despise the overall system. With this resent there comes a natural instinct to rebel against it. For some reason this is especially true for boys and girls do not seem to be effected much by it, they just get on with it. This makes up what happened last year when the boys did on average a lot worse than the girls in their exams.

Pupils should be able to do their work whenever they want. They turn up to school and they go to lessons as usual. However unlike at the moment, all work should be done on state of the art laptop computers, which should be issued at the start of each pupil's school career. These laptops should be able to link up via optical cables to the desks, in each classroom and, then a local campus wide intra-net links all the terminals. Each classroom has a master code which only teachers have. Therefore the teachers would be able to teach and keep an eye on what each pupil is doing. Also if a teacher were off sick they would still be able to take the lesson giving the pupils instructions by some sort of instant messaging program over the Internet.

Then the part where teenagers would really see the difference. At the back of each classroom there would be a little one way sound proof common room. In the common room there would be terminals to the overall school intra-net where pupils would be able to see what has happened and what is going to be covered in all the subjects. This way pupils would really be able to do whatever subject they wanted to do at whatever time they wanted. Also in the common rooms there would be vending machines. If the pupils really felt like time out then there would be a door to the outside world so they could just get up and leave if they wanted. It wouldn't matter about kids wandering about in-between lessons, as the classrooms would be sound proofed.

There would be votes involving whole years to decide what changes should be made to the school i.e. colour schemes in classrooms and corridors. What to put into common rooms. Each year would be given two common rooms for different schemes. For example one room may be silent then the other have a huge hi-fi with huge 500 watt speakers. The schools would provide all. Theft would not be a problem, as all the children would hopefully realize how privileged they were. Some rooms, mainly specified common rooms would permit graffiti. So that students did not graffiti the other rooms and things like tables and chairs. Also some of the minorities would really appreciate the atmosphere, as they would be able to choose it. For example Goths might choose to congregate in a really dark and mysterious common room. Also around the campus would be such things as small (but not too small) skate parks.

Children would start school six months after you can talk quite fluently in English. Around two and a half years of age. Then during the morning the teachers would talk to you in a foreign language of your parent's choice. You would be taught to read and write in these languages and taught basic maths in these languages too. Then in the afternoon you would be taught your lessons in English. The idea behind this is to make as many children as possible bi-lingual as this would really help their education. The reason for starting education so early is because the younger the child is the more receptive they are to new ideas and information. Of course the younger children wouldn't work as hard as the older children, also they would be taught to write the conventional way before they were moved on to word processing. They would not receive their laptop until they were 6 years old. Also of course the younger children would not be given the same independence as the older children. So the little kids would not just be able to just up and leave the classroom. Also you would have to do the work as it is set, so you would not be able to carry on work from class at home. Homework would be ABOLISHED (ha ha ha) sucks to all the teachers that like to see our tired faces from staying up all night doing homework. There would be as few rules as there would be possible to have. However the few rules there would be would be very strictly regulated. Corporal punishment would be reintroduced for the severest of punishments. The other punishments would be pretty harsh though. The younger kids would be shown the severity of the punishments so that they would learn from the older kid's mistakes and the rules would be drilled into them. This would seriously dissuade them from breaking the rules when they were older and at their worst to handle. However school life should be made as pleasant as possible so there should not be any reason for breaking the rules in the first place.

Feargal, Secondary, Coventry

I would be delighted if I had a dream school with pretty teachers, polite children, bright colours, good displays and a pretty hall with red, blue, green, yellow, pink, brown, purple and with black and silver, gold and orange (walls) and equipment for the playground like a scooter, pretend car, rocking horses and lots more new books and nice colours like red. Do not drop litter and I want nice green trees and we get to wear anything. I'd like trying carving wood off trees and separate desks. I'd paint the bin and have two ponds in the quad.

Cameron, 6, Birmingham

∽∽∽

I wish I had to go to a school where children can slide down slides and a bouncy castle for a classroom, a chocolate teacher for a real teacher and a sweet fountain for a water fountain. There is a room where you can go in and say a title of a story and it will make you be a person in the story plus you're in the story. You can go on to the internet and enter competitions and quizzes and win fun things. There is a room where you can go back in time or into the future.

Samuel, 7, Coventry

∽∽∽

Why do we have to do exams and tests?
Why do they teach us, those ignorant pests?
Why is the building short and tubby?
Why is the Head teacher like Mr Blobby?
Why isn't the playground cool and fun?
Why aren't you allowed to run?
Why are the lessons so boring?
Why does everyone keep on snoring?
Why aren't there any toys?
Why are there so many boys?
Oh no here comes Mr Blobby!

Laura, 7, Halesowen

∽∽∽

I would like if we had to carry on everyday and if we were allowed outside without a coat and if we were allowed on the grass and all we had for break is fruit because it is good for you, and I wish that there were parties everyday and to write more stories and paint more and if there were no classroom rules.

Lee, 7, Londonderry

∽∽∽

I like my school, it's very cool, it's fun and clean, it's never cold or bitter. There are glass pencils. It is really fun. There is brick desks and pools and a huge play ground and good teachers.

Harry, 8, Whitley Bay

∽∽∽

In my dream school I would like a jungle playgroup. Also I would like a tree house for the jungle. But it would be nice there with an eating room, one for boys, one for girls. I think it would be better if we come to school at 12.00 o'clock.

In lessons we could go outside for walks in groups at a time. We should also have rooms for every lesson and subjects. We should do more making stuff out of things people don't use anymore.

We shouldn't have to wear uniform everyday. I want to have lessons every day because nearly everyone likes it. I would like to go on lots of school trips in my dream school. For naughty behaviour it's going to have cameras to take pictures of them. It would be better in my dream school if it had a door bell for each room. I want the school to have a shape of a U.F.O. with lights outside.

Tony, 9, Norwich

The school I'd like to learn at would be to have:
Modernised classrooms
With marble tables
Spaced in a specific manner.
There would be comfortable chairs
With pillows or cushions.
It would have wide windows
With a scenery that can be seen
Far past the ocean
Luxurious treats for when we get tired
After working so hard.
Teachers with respect
Who have manners
And who don't always make the decisions!

Tazim, 12, London

We could start to make a Dream School now. Some of our ideas cost a lot of money which we haven't got. Some of our ideas don't cost nothing so we could start to do them now and make a better school. All the things we don't want people to do like fighting and racists and swearing and bullying don't cost anything. Us and the teachers will have to work hard to make it a better and a happier school. We know it's important that we should be involved in making the Dream School not just the teachers.

Imran, Robert, Nathan, Emma, Qamer, Gohar, Gary, Zahir, Leona, Shazir, Sheridan, Matthew, Kirsty and Mandeep, 13–15, Huddersfield

I feel that this country has the power to change this and to fulfil the hopes of children all around the world . . . Education will not get worse. It has a good future.

James, 12, Loughborough

Afterword

Dea Birkett
Writer, the *Guardian* newspaper

I opened the paper at breakfast this morning. The number of educational issues raised in just one day was astounding: Are exams causing children too much stress? Can creationism be taught in schools? How can literacy rates be raised? Should classroom assistants be given a teaching role? Is there a place for private sector firms in public sector schooling? Each story reported a new solution, a new approach, a new initiative, but every solution was proposed by an adult. I doubt if any of them will work.

If only these adult decision-makers had riffled through the entries for a 'School I'd Like'. They would have had access to over 15,000 voices of individual children, expressing their concerns and ideas about the future of education. Amongst those entries, many of the solutions these adults seek are to be found.

We have ignored children's input to their own future at our peril. In the first 1967 'School I'd Like' competition, most entrants clearly came out against exams. Their plea was ignored; instead of the burden of testing being eased over the last thirty and more years, it has consistently grown and become even more entrenched. So here we are, still stuck with that same old exam question popping up in our papers almost every week – are exams an efficient and equitable way of assessing a student's progress? We continue to ask every expert, except the real experts – the children.

As I riffled through the 2001 competition entries, I was surprised not only by how innovative and imaginative the suggestions on all subjects were, but how solid and sensible. In these children's essays, poems, videos, paintings and songs, there are answers to practically every dilemma that the education system is currently grappling with. Take truancy, for example. There is much discussion today over how to increase school attendance records, and who is to blame if a child doesn't turn up to class. Should the child or the parent be punished? And how? But if we look at these children's competition entries, a continual thread is an intense desire to go to school. Few want no school; the vast majority envisage a school they really want to go to. At their ideal educational establishment, every child would be eager to attend. I would have thought the message from these entries is clear: truancy can't be tackled by punishing anybody – parent or child. The way to tackle truancy is to make schools places that children rush to each morning, excitedly scrambling towards their desks. As primary pupil Sarah Noyce summed up, she wished her dream school would come true, 'So if I had a choice of going to school or staying at home I'd definitely choose to go to school. And I hope if it was really made it would encourage more children to want to come to school.'

Perhaps it is easy to dismiss and sideline what the children say because many make sweeping statements and outline grandiose plans. How could these impossible dreams be put into practice? But the children have also asked for small and easily achievable changes, something as simple as slightly quieter school bells. Surely we could manage to institute just some of them?

But while we become heady with the radicalism of the vast majority of children's views, we must also respect the more conservative minority. Lower secondary students' preoccupation with safety – demanding security systems and CCTV – may be statistically unfounded; schools are still relatively safe havens for children. But these fears shouldn't be dismissed as ridiculous or extreme. Calls for caning bullies, or all-girls schools with free lipsticks on offer with each school meal cannot be laughed at and pushed to one side. If we consult, we must listen, whatever solutions are given and however much it is contrary to what we may have hoped to hear.

Of course, a competition is not scientific research. (But then, neither is a focus group, and they have determined much of government policy.) But over 15,000 children must be one of the largest, if not the largest, informal surveys of children's attitudes towards schooling ever conducted in this country.

I hope those in power listen to this vast voice – not only teachers, heads and local educational authorities, but those above and beyond. The policy-makers at national level should pay heed to those for whom they are planning. There is one lesson that needs to be learnt: unless the children are behind your initiatives, they cannot succeed. A good education cannot be imposed, but has to be understood and embraced by those it is intended to benefit. Children are extraordinarily keen to share the burden of responsibility for examining the future of education. As John Clifford, a winner in the original 1967 competition, said: 'It proves yet again that young people are not a problem that needs to be corralled and curfewed, but an incredible rich resource of wisdom and creative thinking that we should learn to listen to.'

Perhaps this should be the main lesson adults learn from 'The School I'd Like'. Not to adopt any specific proposals, building modifications, or even attempt a new school ethos – although all of these would be nice. But the first lesson must be in listening, and respecting what we hear. Children are so obviously more than ready to take up the challenge of redesigning their education. Are we ready to meet the challenge of listening to them?

This is a book about giving children a voice, so a child must be given the last word – lower secondary school pupil Aleksi Hastings, – who had his entry set as a task by his teacher. His entry began: 'Hi, this is a homework that will probably just be written, read and returned, with a mark and someone's red pen all over it. Yet, I will write this thing anyway.' It ended: 'Please don't just push this aside as another homework, treat this piece presented before you as an academic breakthrough. Goodbye – and make the dream come true.'